# GREAT AMERICAN STORIES 3

Longman

longman.com

**C.G. Draper**

Great American Stories 3: An ESL/EFL Reader

Pearson Education, 10 Bank Street, White Plains, NY 10606

Vice president, director of publishing: Allen Ascher
Acquisitions editor: Laura Le Dréan
Senior development manager: Penny Laporte
Development editors: Paula H. Van Ells, Stacey Hunter
Vice president, director of design and production: Rhea Banker
Executive managing editor: Linda Moser
Associate production editor: Michael Goldberg
Production supervisor: Ray Keating
Director of manufacturing: Patrice Fraccio
Senior manufacturing buyer: Dave Dickey
Cover design: Elizabeth Carlson
Cover image: Images.com/Spots on the Spot/Herzberg, Tom
Text design: Jill Yutkowitz
Text composition: Monika Popowitz
Text art: Charles Shaw

**Library of Congress Cataloging-in-Publication Data**
Great American stories 3 / [compiled by] C.G. Draper.
    p. cm.
  Contents: Breakfast / John Steinbeck-- A day's wait / Ernest Hemingway -- April
showers / Edith Wharton -- Rip van Winkle / Washington Irving -- The wives of the
dead / Nathaniel Hawthorne - - Nine needles / James Thurber -- A mystery of
heroism / Stephen Crane -- A visit of charity / Eudora Welty -- The black ball /
Ralph Ellison.
  ISBN 0-13-061941-8 (alk. paper)
  1. English language -- Textbooks for foreign speakers. 2. Short stories,
American -- Adaptations. 3. Readers -- United States. I. Title: Great American
stories three. II. Draper, C.G.

PE1128 .G6568 2002
428.6'4--dc21                                                2002075480

Printed in the United States of America
2 3 4 5 6 7 8 9 10–CRW–06 05 04 03 02

# CONTENTS

# TO THE TEACHER

GREAT AMERICAN STORIES 3 consists of nine stories by classic American writers with language development exercises for each story in reading skills, vocabulary development, writing, and discussion. Prereading exercises introduce the student to the world of the story and help develop the student's reading skills in scanning and skimming. One of the prereading exercises in each chapter is based on the biographical information about each author given on the title page of the story. These biographical paragraphs are also often a basis for the scanning and skimming exercises, and for the language activity and writing exercises in the final chapter.

Five of the stories in the book are unabridged, and four have been carefully adapted from the originals. Both the content of the stories and the demands of the exercises gradually increase in difficulty from the first story, which is at the upper intermediate level of proficiency, to the last, which is at the advanced level. Standard headword lists and structural controls were used in selecting the stories, in adapting those that required adaptation, and in arranging their order within the book.

A major aim of this book is to help the student develop the skill of understanding vocabulary in context—that is, of guessing the meaning of a word using the context clues that surround it in its own sentence or in the sentences that precede or follow it. This skill, though important at all levels of language acquisition, is especially needed by students who are approaching advanced levels of proficiency and encountering for the first time unabridged texts of some sophistication and complexity. Opportunities for the teacher to encourage the development of this "guessing" skill abound throughout the book but are the special focus of two sections in each chapter: the *Key Words* paragraph and the exercise *Understanding Words in Context*. The *Key Words* paragraph that immediately precedes each story gives a brief introduction to the story using several words that are basic to the reader's understanding of the material. Each word (in **boldface** in the paragraph) is at least partially defined by phrases or synonyms within the paragraph.

The exercise *Understanding Words in Context* uses different techniques to expand the student's awareness of context as an aid in determining a word's meaning. In addition, several of the *Close Reading* and *Vocabulary Practice* exercises reinforce the importance of context to comprehension. Given this emphasis in the book, the teacher would do well, before beginning, to introduce the students to the broad concept of understanding words in context.

Students should try to read each story in one sitting and immediately attempt to answer the questions in the first postreading exercise, *Understanding the Plot*. If the student has trouble with this exercise, he or she should be asked to repeat it after completing the next two exercises, *Understanding Words in Context* and *Close Reading*, which require rereading of key sections of the story. The first reading "stretches" the student; the exercises and rereadings consolidate gains and help the student achieve complete familiarity with the material.

GREAT AMERICAN STORIES 3 is designed to be incorporated into a twelve- to fourteen-week course as part of the reading program. The materials can be used in or out of class—as a core reading text, ancillary text, or pleasure reading. In class, it can be used interactively, with the teacher leading the discussion or with the students working in pairs or small groups. Because the stories, biographical paragraphs, and exercises introduce the student to important people and periods in American cultural, social, and political history, the book can also be used as a springboard for further study or research.

C.G.D.

# TO THE READER

This book starts at the upper intermediate level and ends at the advanced level. The book contains nine stories with exercises that increase in difficulty throughout the book. Working on them will help you enlarge your vocabulary and improve your skills in reading, writing, speaking, and discussion.

Each chapter begins with a paragraph about the life of the author. Short exercises follow, with questions about that paragraph, about the illustrations (pictures) that go with the story, and about the general subject or theme of the story. You will also complete an exercise that helps you develop special reading skills. Finally, before reading the story itself, you will read a short paragraph that introduces the story and some key words that you need to know before you begin reading.

Each story is followed first by the exercise Understanding the Plot. This exercise checks your basic understanding of the story. If you have trouble completing it, you should continue on to the next two exercises, which guide your rereading of sentences and paragraphs central to the meaning of the story. After another reading of the story, you should be able to complete Understanding the Plot with ease.

The second exercise following the story is Understanding Words in Context. This exercise will help you develop the important skill of guessing the meaning of a word that is new to you. The word *context* here means the words or phrases that come just before or after a new word and help determine its exact meaning. These words or phrases are context clues—that is, signs that point to, and help you understand, the meaning of the new word. Several of the Close Reading and Vocabulary Practice exercises also use context as a tool for comprehension.

The stories in this book were written in the nineteenth and twentieth centuries by nine of America's most famous writers. In reading their stories and learning something about their lives, you will be introduced to important people and periods in American cultural, social, and political history.

C.G.D.

# *1*

# BREAKFAST

❋

### A story by
### JOHN STEINBECK

John Steinbeck was born in 1902 in Salinas, California. He grew up in a farming valley surrounded by mountains, about a hundred miles south of San Francisco and twenty-five miles from the Pacific Coast. The valley, the mountains, and the coast serve as settings for many of Steinbeck's best and most famous stories. His mother, a schoolteacher, encouraged him to read widely as a child. After taking many courses but no degree from Stanford University, Steinbeck held a variety of jobs that developed in him a deep sympathy for the life of working people. In the 1930s, a time of great economic hardship, Steinbeck wrote five books that became the basis of his future fame. They are *Tortilla Flat* (1935), *In Dubious Battle* (1936), *Of Mice and Men* (1937), *The Long Valley* (1938), a collection of stories from which "Breakfast" is taken, and *The Grapes of Wrath* (1939), a long novel about farming families that many consider his best. Steinbeck's writing is straightforward, natural, and clear, but expresses great emotion beneath its simple surface. Steinbeck published more than thirty books during his productive career; many of his stories were made into films. In 1962, he won the Nobel Prize for literature. He died in 1968.

# BEFORE YOU READ THE STORY

## A. About the Author

Read the paragraph about John Steinbeck on page 1. Where are many of Steinbeck's stories set? What did Steinbeck's various jobs develop in him?

## B. The Picture

Read the **Key Words** paragraph on page 3. How many of the boldface words in that paragraph can you identify in the picture on page 6?

## C. Thinking About Hard Times

"Breakfast" takes place during the 1930s, a period of great economic hardship in the United States and throughout the world. The main characters in the story are poor workers who move from farm to farm looking for jobs. They have few possessions and little education (their English, as you will see, is "nonstandard" —that is, very informal and sometimes ungrammatical). It is a struggle for them to make enough money to take care of the simplest human needs. What do you think are some of the things that give people pleasure during hard times? What are some of the things that bring you happiness during times of difficulty?

## D. Scanning for Information

Reading quickly to find small pieces of information is called *scanning*. In this exercise you will scan the section "To the Reader" on page vi and the Key Words paragraph on page 3. When you are scanning "To the Reader," let your eyes move quickly over the text until you find the phrase "Understanding Words in Context." Then read closely enough to answer the following questions.

1. What is the "context" of a new word?
2. What does the "context" help you to understand?
3. What are "context clues"?
4. In the Key Words paragraph on page 3, what words or phrases are the "context clues" that help you understand each word in boldface?

"Breakfast" takes place in an outdoor camp near California farmland. The camp is simple, consisting of a tent, an old **iron stove** for cooking, a **packing box** used as a table, no chairs, and a few **tin cups** and plates. Four people are living in the camp: a young woman and her baby, a young man, and an older man. They are farm workers, and they have recently found work **picking cotton**—that is, taking cotton off the plant by hand. The woman is dressed in an old, washed-out skirt and a blouse or shirt; the men wear **dungarees**, clothing made of rough dark-blue cotton (blue jeans). They are about to eat a breakfast of coffee, bacon, and **biscuits**—quickly made bread baked in a pan in small round shapes.

# BREAKFAST

This thing fills me with pleasure. I don't know why, I can see it in the smallest detail. I find myself recalling it again and again, each time bringing more detail out of sunken memory; remembering brings the curious warm pleasure.

2      It was very early in the morning. The eastern mountains were black-blue, but behind them the light stood up faintly colored at the mountain rims with a washed red, growing colder, greyer and darker as it went up and overhead until, at a place near the west, it merged with pure night.

3      And it was cold, not painfully so, but cold enough so that I rubbed my hands and shoved them deep into my pockets, and I hunched my shoulders up and scuffled my feet on the ground. Down in the valley where I was, the earth was that lavender[1] grey of dawn. I walked along a country road and ahead of me I saw a tent that was only a little lighter grey than the ground. Beside the tent there was a flash of orange fire seeping out of the cracks of an old rusty iron stove. Grey smoke spurted up out of the stubby

---

[1] lavender = light purple

stovepipe, spurted up a long way before it spread out and dissipated.

4      I saw a young woman beside the stove, really a girl. She was dressed in a faded cotton skirt and waist.[2]  As I came close I saw that she carried a baby in a crooked arm and the baby was nursing,[3] its head under her waist out of the cold. The mother moved about, poking the fire, shifting the rusty lids of the stove to make a greater draft, opening the oven door; and all the time the baby was nursing, but that didn't interfere with the mother's work, nor with the light quick gracefulness of her movements. There was something very precise and practiced in her movements. The orange fire flicked out of the cracks in the stove and threw dancing reflections on the tent.

5      I was close now and I could smell frying bacon and baking bread, the warmest, pleasantest odors I know. From the east the light grew swiftly. I came near to the stove and stretched my hands out to it and shivered all over when the warmth struck me.  Then the tent flap jerked up and a young man came out and an older man followed him. They were dressed in new blue dungarees and in new dungaree coats with brass buttons shining.  They were sharp-faced men, and they looked much alike.

6      The younger had a dark stubble beard and the older had a grey stubble beard.  Their heads and faces were wet, their hair dripped with water, and water stood out on their stiff beards and their cheeks shone with water.  Together they stood looking quietly at the lightening east; they yawned together and looked at the light on the hill rims. They turned and saw me.

7      "Morning," said the older man.  His face was neither friendly nor unfriendly.

8      "Morning, sir," I said.

9      "Morning," said the young man.

10      The water was slowly drying on their faces.  They came to the stove and warmed their hands at it.

11      The girl kept to her work, her face averted and her eyes on what she was doing.  Her hair was tied back out of her eyes with a string and it hung down her back and swayed as

---

[2] waist = a shirt or blouse that comes to the waist: the upper part of a woman's dress.
[3] nursing = being breast-fed by its mother

she worked. She set tin cups on a big packing box, set tin plates and knives and forks out too. Then she scooped fried bacon out of the deep grease and laid it on a big tin platter, and the bacon clicked and rustled as it grew crisp. She opened the rusty oven door and took out a square pan full of high big biscuits.

12    When the smell of that hot bread came out, both of the men inhaled deeply. The young man said softly, "Keerist!"[4]

13    The older man turned to me, "Had your breakfast?"

14    "No."

15    "Well, sit down with us, then."

16    That was the signal. We went to the packing case and squatted on the ground about it. The young man asked, "picking cotton?"

17    "No."

18    "We have twelve days' work so far," the young man said.

19    The girl spoke up from the stove. "They even got new clothes."

20    The two men looked down at their new dungarees and they both smiled a little.

21    The girl set out the platter of bacon, the brown high biscuits, a bowl of bacon gravy and a pot of coffee, and then she squatted down by the box too. The baby was still nursing, its head up under her waist out of the cold. I could hear the sucking noises it made.

22    We filled our plates, poured bacon gravy over our biscuits and sugared our coffee. The older man filled his mouth full and he chewed and chewed and swallowed. Then he said, "God Almighty, it's good," and he filled his mouth again.

23    The young man said, "We been eating good for twelve days."

24    We all ate quickly, frantically, and refilled our plates and ate quickly again until we were full and warm. The hot bitter coffee scalded our throats. We threw the last little bit with the grounds in it on the earth and refilled our cups.

25    There was the color of the light now, a reddish gleam that made the air seem colder. The two men faced the east and their faces were lighted by the dawn, and I looked up

---

[4] Keerist (pronounced kee-RICED) = Christ. The man pronounces the word *Christ* in this way to avoid swearing. He wants only to express his satisfaction with the wonderful smell of the bread.

for a moment and saw the image of the mountain and the light coming over it reflected in the older man's eyes.

26    Then the two men threw the grounds from their cups on the earth and they stood up together. "Got to get going," the older man said.

27    The younger man turned to me. "'Fyou want to pick cotton, we could maybe get you on."[5]

28    "No. I got to go along. Thanks for breakfast."

29    The older man waved his hand in a negative. "O.K. Glad to have you." They walked away together. The air was blazing with light at the eastern skyline. And I walked away down the country road.

30    That's all. I know, of course, some of the reasons why it was pleasant. But there was some element of great beauty there that makes the rush of warmth when I think of it.

## AFTER YOU READ THE STORY

### A. Understanding the Plot

Answer the following questions with complete sentences.

1. What time of day was it when the narrator (the person telling the story) saw the tent and the camp? What was the weather like?
2. What were the first things the narrator saw in the camp?
3. What was the young woman doing when the narrator arrived? Who was with her as she worked?
4. In what ways were the two men in the camp similar?
5. What work had the two men been doing lately?
6. What did the men and the woman have for breakfast?
7. After breakfast, what did the younger man invite the narrator to do, and what was the narrator's response?
8. When the narrator thinks back on that early-morning scene, what are his feelings?

---

[5] If you want to pick cotton, maybe we could get you a job.

## B. Understanding Words in Context

Each of the following items has a word from the story followed by the number of the paragraph and the phrase in which it appears. Without using a dictionary, guess the meaning of the word from its context. If necessary, reread the paragraph more closely. Then complete the sentence that follows, choosing the ending that best demonstrates the meaning of the word.

Example: *merge (2) . . . the light . . . at a place near the west . . . merged with pure night.*

When the two rivers merged, they
    a. broke into many separate streams.
   (b.) joined together into one river.
    c. remained separate but strong.

1. *shove (3) . . . I rubbed my hands and shoved them deep into my pockets.*

   When he saw the bus coming, he shoved the test papers into his book bag,
   a. wanting to keep them perfect to show his parents.
   b. not caring if they got folded or torn.
   c. even though this took so much time that he missed the bus.

2. *seep (3) . . . there was a flash of orange fire seeping out of the cracks . . .*

   When the dark oil started seeping out of the ground, the oilman
   a. jumped back quickly to avoid getting splashed with it.
   b. watched with joy as it shot up into the sky.
   c. watched it slowly gather until he was sure what it was.

3. *poke (4) The mother moved about, poking the fire . . .*

   When the girl began poking the boy in front of her with her pencil,
   a. he began crying because of the heat.
   b. he turned around and shouted at her.
   c. the teacher thanked her for her help.

4. *shift (4)  The mother moved about . . . <u>shifting</u> the rusty lids of the stove . . .*

We <u>shifted</u> the furniture in our living room
   **a.** and made more space near the fireplace.
   **b.** and burned the pieces in the fireplace.
   **c.** and spent the money on a new fireplace.

5. *yawn (6) . . . they <u>yawned</u> together and looked at the light on the hill rims.*

After the politicians had argued the point for an hour, I <u>yawned</u>
   **a.** because I had grown sleepy.
   **b.** because my anger was uncontrollable.
   **c.** because I was thinking so deeply about the issues.

6. *sway (11)  Her hair . . . hung down her back and <u>swayed</u> as she worked.*

The tall old tree started <u>swaying</u>
   **a.** when the sun lit it up.
   **b.** when the wind blew strongly.
   **c.** when the soft snow began falling.

7. *squat (16)  We went to the packing case and <u>squatted</u> on the ground about it.*

While giving directions to his friends, the boy suddenly <u>squatted</u>
   **a.** at the distant mountains, and the others turned their eyes to follow him.
   **b.** and then fell asleep right there where he lay.
   **c.** and drew a map in the dirt with a stick.

8. *scald (24)  The hot bitter coffee <u>scalded</u> our throats.*

To make sure the milk for her baby wasn't <u>scalding</u>, the mother
   **a.** gave some to the cat to drink first.
   **b.** shook some drops of it onto the back of her hand.
   **c.** drank more water than usual for a few days.

## C. Close Reading: Simplicity

Steinbeck uses simple words and a simple situation to create a special mood in "Breakfast." Show how he achieves this effect by answering the questions below using words and phrases taken from the story. Paragraph numbers are given to guide your rereading.

**Example:** *Steinbeck fills the beginning of his story with colors. What are some of them, and what do they describe? (2–3)*

<u>black-blue mountains...washed red light...dark grey light overhead...lavender grey earth...orange fire...grey smoke...</u>

1. What words does Steinbeck use to describe the movements of the young woman who is making breakfast and feeding her baby at the same time? (4)

   _____

2. How do the men react to the taste of the simple breakfast? (21–24)

   _____

3. How does the stranger "introduce" himself to the family in the camp? (5–9)

   _____

4. How does the older man of the family in the camp react to the stranger? (7–10, 13–15)

   _____

5. What kind of clothes are the men wearing, and what do they seem to think about their clothes? (5, 19–20)

   _____

6. After breakfast, the light is coming up. How does Steinbeck show the connection between the farm workers and the beauty of nature? (25)

   _____

## D. Vocabulary Practice

Choose the word from the list below that is closest in meaning to the underlined word or phrase in each sentence. Write it in the space provided. The paragraph in which the word appears is given in parentheses.

recall (1)       sunken (1)       spurted (3)       dissipate (3)
gracefulness (4)   swiftly (5)     shiver (5)        averted (11)

1. It was not fear that made him <u>shake</u> when he stood near the stove, but his body's memory of the cold. _____

2. Would he <u>remember</u> an experience like this "again and again" unless it gave him pleasure? _____

3. If she <u>turned</u> her eyes <u>away</u>, it was from shyness, not dislike. _____

4. She was cooking over a rusty stove; but the <u>smooth and attractive movements</u> of the young woman got his attention. _____

5. Like many other images from the distant past, this one was <u>lying deep down</u> in the narrator's memory. _____

6. Like the grey smoke rising from the stove, the clouds slowly began to <u>break up and disappear</u> as the sun grew in strength. _____

7. How <u>fast</u> the morning came! Before they knew it, it was time to leave for work. _____

8. The smoke that <u>rushed forcefully out</u> from the stove looked like water from an underground spring. _____

## E. Word Forms

A participle is a verb form ending in *–ing* (present) or *–ed* (past). It can be used as an adjective. The present participle is active; the noun it describes performs an action (*the rushing waters*). The past participle is passive; it describes a quality or state given *to* the noun (*the rushed dinner*).

| Present Participle | Past Participle |
|---|---|
| flashing | flashed |
| gleaming | gleamed |
| rushing | rushed |
| shivering | shivered |
| stretching | stretched |

Complete the sentences with the present or past participles of the verb given.

1. *(flash)* He was arrested after he drove his car straight through the _____ red light.

2. *(gleam)* I wanted to have the same _____ teeth as the woman in the advertisement, so I bought a tube of Snow toothpaste.

3. *(rush)* I felt so _____ during the test that I began to panic and couldn't finish.

4. *(shiver)* She wrapped the _____ girl in a blanket and brought her closer to the fire.

5. *(stretch)* The bear's skin, _____ and dried, made clothing for the early hunters.

## F. Discussion: "Some of the reasons why it was pleasant."

Before starting this exercise, reread the first and last paragraphs of "Breakfast."

1. The first words of the story are "this thing," and the last word is "it." By the end of the story, do we know what these words refer to?
2. Make a list of at least five things that you believe gave pleasure to the narrator during his visit to the camp. Then discuss your list with two other students. Combine the three different lists into one list. How many items does the final list contain?
3. Think about the "element of great beauty" that the narrator mentions in the last paragraph. What is it? Summarize it in a few words.
4. Where do you think the narrator might have been coming from at the start of the story? Where do you think he might be going at the end of it?

## G. Language Activity: The Great Depression

In the United States, the worldwide economic disaster of the 1930s is called the Great Depression. (The word *depression* in this economic context means "a period in which many businesses fail and many people are unemployed.")

1. Find information about the Great Depression using one or more of the following sources:

   - an encyclopedia (look under the heading "Great Depression")
   - an information website (a "search engine") on the Internet (use the search phrase "Great Depression")
   - something an older person told you or someone close to you about life during those difficult years

Take notes as you search for the information. From your source or sources, try to find answers to some of the following questions:

- What happened to employment (that is, jobs) during the Great Depression?
- How did the lives of many people change?
- How did the poorest people get food to eat?
- What happened to those who could find no way to support their families?
- What caused the Great Depression? When did it end?

2. Organize the notes you took during your search. Choose a few subjects (for example, "causes," "employment," "effect on families," "government actions") and group your notes under these subjects. Prepare a short, informal oral report on one of your subjects for the class. Do not write down and read your report; speak from the notes you took.

## H. Writing: A One-Paragraph Report

Using the notes you took for Exercise G, write a one-paragraph report of 75–125 words on the Great Depression. Try to organize your paragraph around one main idea or topic, such as "the main causes of the Great Depression" or "the effect of the Great Depression on farmers" or "family life during the Great Depression." The first sentence of your paragraph should be a general statement that introduces and summarizes your main topic.

# 2

# A DAY'S WAIT

✵

A story by
## ERNEST HEMINGWAY

Ernest Hemingway was born in Oak Park, Illinois in 1899. His father, a doctor, encouraged his love of the outdoor life of camping, fishing, and hunting. As a boy he spent summer vacations in the woods of upper Michigan, which later became the setting for some of his best-known stories. In World War I, Hemingway offered his services as a Red Cross ambulance driver, and in 1918 he was seriously wounded in Italy. Three of his best novels—*The Sun Also Rises* (1926), *A Farewell to Arms* (1929), and *For Whom the Bell Tolls* (1940)—take place in Europe during or after a war. Indeed, war, as a personal experience and as a general condition of human life, is central to most of Hemingway's writing. Many of his characters are fighting a battle that was lost before they began fighting. What is important to Hemingway is the way the characters behave in that battle and how they face the difficulties of life. Hemingway's short stories have influenced generations of American writers. Much of the meaning in his stories lies under the surface of his clean, clear writing style. His object, he once wrote, was to "make people feel something more than they understood." He lived most of his last years in Cuba, and his adventures as a hunter and journalist were widely reported. After publishing his famous short novel *The Old Man and the Sea* in 1952, Hemingway was awarded the Pulitzer Prize (1953) and the Nobel Prize for literature (1954). He left Cuba in 1960, moved to Idaho, and in 1961 ended his own life by shooting himself.

**15**

## BEFORE YOU READ THE STORY

### A. About the Author

Read the paragraph about Ernest Hemingway on page 15. What in his personal life may have caused him to write frequently about war? What did you learn from the paragraph about Hemingway's writing style?

### B. The Pictures

In the picture on page 18, the small round objects on the table next to the boy's bed are pills, or **capsules**. Why do you think the boy is in bed? In the picture on page 19, the man is hunting **quail**—small birds that nest on the ground. The dog beside him is an **Irish setter**, a kind of hunting dog. What time of year is it?

### C. Thinking About Childhood Fears

When you were a child, were you ever frightened by something you didn't understand? What was it? Were you ever frightened by something you understood incorrectly (that is, you thought you understood it, but you were wrong)? What was it?

### D. Scanning Two Sources of Information

Sometimes we need to scan two sources of information quickly for the purpose of making a comparison between two people, things, or ideas. Using the paragraphs about Hemingway on page 15 and Steinbeck on page 1, compare the two writers by answering the questions below. Try to complete the exercise in less than three minutes.

1. Which writer lived the longest?
2. Where did each of the two writers set many of their stories?
3. What subject or subjects did each writer often write about?
4. In what way were the writing styles of the two writers similar?
5. Which writer won the Nobel Prize for literature?

"A Day's Wait" is about a nine-year-old boy who is sick with **influenza**—an illness (often called "the flu") that includes high temperature, or **fever**, among its symptoms. Any of the different forms of the disease can become an **epidemic** in a community, spreading among many of the community's members. The flu can be dangerous if it leads to **pneumonia**, a condition in which the lungs fill with liquid, making breathing difficult. The boy and his father are Americans living in Europe. The story is told by the boy's father, who calls his son "**Schatz**"—a German word meaning "treasure" and often used as an affectionate nickname.

# A DAY'S WAIT

He came into the room to shut the windows while we were still in bed and I saw he looked ill. He was shivering, his face was white, and he walked slowly as though it ached to move.

2    "What's the matter, Schatz?"

3    "I've got a headache."

4    "You better go back to bed."

5    "No. I'm all right."

6    "You go to bed. I'll see you when I'm dressed."

7    But when I came downstairs he was dressed, sitting by the fire, looking a very sick and miserable boy of nine years. When I put my hand on his forehead I knew he had a fever.

8    "You go up to bed," I said, "you're sick."

9    "I'm all right," he said.

10    When the doctor came he took the boy's temperature.

11    "What is it?" I asked him.

12    "One hundred and two."

13    Downstairs, the doctor left three different medicines in different colored capsules with instructions for giving them.

One was to bring down the fever, another a purgative,[1] the third to overcome an acid condition. The germs of influenza can only exist in an acid condition, he explained. He seemed to know all about influenza and said there was nothing to worry about if the fever did not go above one hundred and four degrees. This was a light epidemic of flu and there was no danger if you avoided pneumonia.

14      Back in the room I wrote the boy's temperature down and made a note of the time to give the various capsules.

15      "Do you want me to read to you?"

16      "All right. If you want to," said the boy. His face was very white and there were dark areas under his eyes. He lay still in the bed and seemed very detached from what was going on.

17      I read aloud from Howard Pyle's *Book of Pirates*; but I could see he was not following what I was reading.

---

[1] purgative = a medicine that cleans out the body.

18  "How do you feel, Schatz?" I asked him.

19  "Just the same, so far," he said.

20  I sat at the foot of the bed and read to myself while I waited for it to be time to give another capsule. It would have been natural for him to go to sleep, but when I looked up he was looking at the foot of the bed, looking very strangely.

21  "Why don't you try to sleep? I'll wake you up for the medicine."

22  "I'd rather stay awake."

23  After awhile he said to me, "You don't have to stay in here with me, Papa, if it bothers you."

24  "It doesn't bother me."

25  "No, I mean you don't have to stay if it's going to bother you."

26  I thought perhaps he was a little lightheaded and after giving him the prescribed capsules at eleven o'clock I went out for a while.

27  It was a bright, cold day, the ground covered with a sleet that had frozen so that it seemed as if all the bare trees, the bushes, the cut brush and all the grass and the bare ground had been varnished with ice. I took the young Irish setter for a little walk up the road and along a frozen creek, but it was difficult to stand or walk on the glassy surface and the red dog slipped and slithered and I fell twice, hard, once dropping my gun and having it slide away over the ice.

28  We flushed a covey[2] of quail under a high clay bank with overhanging brush and I killed two as they went out of sight over the top of the bank. Some of the covey lit[3] in trees, but most of them scattered into brush piles and it was necessary to jump on the ice-coated mounds of brush several times before they would flush. Coming out while you were poised unsteadily on the icy, springy brush they made difficult shooting[4] and I killed two, missed five, and started back pleased to have found a covey close to the house and happy there were so many left to find another day.

---

[2] covey = a small group of birds
[3] lit = in this context, the word means "came down and settled"
[4] they made difficult shooting = they made shooting difficult

29    At the house they said the boy had refused to let anyone come into the room.

30    "You can't come in," he said. "You mustn't get what I have."

31    I went up to him and found him in exactly the position I had left him, white-faced, but with the tops of his cheeks flushed by the fever, staring still, as he had stared, at the foot of the bed.

32    I took his temperature.

33    "What is it?"

34    "Something like a hundred," I said. It was one hundred and two and four tenths.

35    "It was a hundred and two," he said.

36    "Who said so?"

37    "The doctor."

38     "Your temperature is all right," I said. "It's nothing to worry about."

39     "I don't worry," he said, "but I can't keep from thinking."

40     "Don't think," I said. "Just take it easy."

41     "I'm taking it easy," he said and looked straight ahead. He was evidently holding tight onto himself about something.

42     "Take this with water."

43     "Do you think it will do any good?"

44     "Of course it will."

45     I sat down and opened the *Pirate* book and commenced to read, but I could see he was not following, so I stopped.

46     "About what time do you think I'm going to die?" he asked.

47     "What?"

48     "About how long will it be before I die?"

49     "You aren't going to die. What's the matter with you?"

50     "Oh, yes, I am. I heard him say a hundred and two."

51     "People don't die with a fever of one hundred and two. That's a silly way to talk."

52     "I know they do. At school in France the boys told me you can't live with forty-four degrees. I've got a hundred and two."

53     He had been waiting to die all day, ever since nine o'clock in the morning.

54     "You poor Schatz," I said. "It's like miles and kilometers. You know, like how many kilometers we make when we do seventy miles in the car?"

55     "Oh," he said.

56     But his gaze at the foot of the bed relaxed slowly. The hold over himself relaxed too, finally, and the next day it was very slack[5] and he cried very easily at little things that were of no importance.

---

[5] slack = without energy; weak; soft

## AFTER YOU READ THE STORY

### A. Understanding the Plot

Answer the following questions with complete sentences.

1. Why did the father think that the boy was sick?
2. What was the boy's temperature?
3. Downstairs, when the boy was not listening, what did the doctor say to the father about the boy's temperature?
4. How did the boy behave when his father offered to read to him? How did he behave while his father was reading to him?
5. Before the father went hunting, how serious did he think the boy's condition was?
6. What did the boy think was going to happen to him?
7. When the father explained about kilometers and miles, what did the boy understand?
8. How did the boy behave the next day?

### B. Understanding Words in Context

Carefully reread the story's hunting scene, paragraphs 27 and 28. Although there are difficult sentences and unusual words in these paragraphs, you can determine their meaning by studying context clues. In the sentences or phrases below, guess the meaning of the underlined words without looking at a dictionary. Then choose the one definition that comes closest to the meaning you have guessed. Be prepared to explain what context clues led you to this choice.

**Example:** *It was a bright, cold day, the ground covered with a <u>sleet</u> that had frozen . . .*

    **a.** pile of stones
    **b.** watery coat
    **c.** layer of thin ice

The whole sentence shows us that, whatever *sleet* is, it can be frozen. It seems to cover not only the ground, but also trees, bushes, and grass. And the end of the sentence seems to say that it looks like ice. Therefore, neither "stones" nor something "watery" can be the best answer. Sleet must be something like a layer of thin ice, answer c.

1. *. . . all the bare trees, the bushes, the cut <u>brush</u> . . . most of them scattered into <u>brush</u> piles . . . the ice-coated mounds of <u>brush</u> . . . the icy, springy <u>brush</u> . . .*
   a. branches of small trees and bushes
   b. logs from big trees
   c. finely cut grass

2. *I took the young Irish setter for a little walk up the road and along a frozen <u>creek</u>, but it was difficult to stand or walk on the glassy surface . . .*
   a. hill
   b. stream
   c. waterfall

3. *We <u>flushed</u> a covey of quail . . . it was necessary to jump on the ice-coated mounds of brush several times before they would flush.*
   a. searched for and found
   b. caused to fly upward suddenly
   c. destroyed, killed

4. *Coming out while <u>you</u> were poised unsteadily on the icy, springy brush they made difficult shooting . . .*
   a. the reader
   b. the father's friend
   c. any hunter

5. *. . . I killed <u>two</u>, missed <u>five</u>, and started back . . .*
   a. birds
   b. Irish setters
   c. brush piles

## C. Close Reading: Clues to Character

Until the boy says, "About what time do you think I'm going to die?" (paragraph 46), neither the father nor the reader knows exactly what the boy is thinking. Yet the boy has given us several clues during his long day's wait for death to come. Each quotation from the story below is followed by a statement about the quotation. If the statement is true, write **T** next to it. If it is not true, write **F**, for false. Then, on a separate piece of paper, rewrite the statement to make it true.

**Example:** *"Do you want me to read to you?"*
*"All right. If you want to," said the boy. (15–16)*

   **F**  The boy is making sure that his father really wants to read to him.

(The boy is already beginning to think he might die. He is not paying close attention to his father.)

1. *"How do you feel, Schatz?" I asked him.*
   *"Just the same, so far," he said.* (18–19)

   \_\_\_\_ The words "so far" suggest that the boy thinks he knows what will happen, but it hasn't begun to happen yet.

2. *"Why don't you try to sleep? I'll wake you up for the medicine."*
   *"I'd rather stay awake."* (21–22)

   \_\_\_\_ The boy is saying here that he really isn't sleepy.

3. *After a while he said to me, "You don't have to stay in here with me, Papa, if it bothers you."*
   *"It doesn't bother me."*
   *"No, I mean you don't have to stay if it's going to bother you."* (23–25)

   \_\_\_\_ By "it," the boy means his fever.

4. *"I'm taking it easy," he said and looked straight ahead. He was evidently holding tight onto himself about something. (41)*

   \_\_\_\_ The boy is preparing himself to die.

## D. Vocabulary Practice

From the list of medical terms below, choose a word or phrase that best completes the sentences that follow.

| | | |
|---|---|---|
| influenza or flu | epidemic | pneumonia |
| thermometer | temperature | shiver |
| fever | prescription | ache |

1. One of the first things a doctor does to determine the nature of an illness is to take the patient's _____.

2. To do so, the doctor uses a(n) _____.

3. If this instrument shows higher than 98.6° Fahrenheit (37° Celsius), then the patient is said to have a(n) _____.

4. In such a condition, even though the patient's body temperature is high, he or she can sometimes be seen to _____, as if very cold.

5. At the same time, the patient's whole body can begin to _____, and this pain is not imaginary but real.

6. All of these are typical signs of an illness called _____.

7. When the condition is very serious, the doctor must observe the lungs carefully in case there are signs of possible _____.

8. The doctor is likely to give a(n) _____ for various medicines to be taken by the patient, though usually time, rest, and water are the best cures.

9. Even in modern times, with new technology and improved public health awareness, this serious illness can lead to a(n) _____ in small or even large communities.

## E. Word Forms

Complete the chart with the correct form of the words from the story. Use your dictionary if you need help.

| Noun | Verb | Adjective |
|------|------|-----------|
| commencement | _____ | commencing |
| _____ | detach | detached |
| poise | poise | _____ |
| prescription | _____ | prescribing, prescribed |
| relaxation | relax | _____ |

Now, choose one word from the chart to complete each sentence below.

1. There was no sign of _____ in the way the boy kept a tight hold on himself throughout the day.

2. At the _____ of his illness, the boy claimed to be "all right" and didn't want to go back to bed.

3. The doctor _____ various colored capsules.

4. The father noticed, but did not understand, the boy's _____ from what was going on around him.

5. At one moment during the hunt, the Irish setter was stiffly _____ like an arrow, pointing his nose and tail at the quail.

## F. Discussion: Your Opinions

1. The boy in Hemingway's story is nine years old. Do you think his behavior showed courage or fear? What words would you use to describe his character?

2. What words would you use to describe the father's character?

3. Did you enjoy reading this story? Why, or why not?
4. In general, do you like to read stories about family relationships? Why, or why not? Which do you prefer: stories about adventure and danger, stories about romance, stories that are funny, or true stories? Do you feel the same way about stories told in movies and TV shows?

## G. Language Activity: An Interview about Parents and Children

Interview a classmate to find out what he or she thinks of the relationship between the boy and his father in Hemingway's story. Find out how this relationship compares to other child–parent relationships your classmate is familiar with. You may want to ask your classmate some of the following questions or think of some questions on your own. Take notes during the interview so that you can report on your interview to the whole class.

- Would you describe the boy's relationship with his father as close, or distant, or both? Do you think the relationship is normal or unusual? Why?
- What signs in the story do you see of closeness between the boy and his father? What signs do you see of distance between them?
- Do you see any sign of a mother or other woman in the story? How do you think this affects the relationship between the boy and his father?
- In the story, while the boy is sick, the father goes out hunting, and his mind seems not to be on his sick child at all. Do you think this father's behavior is typical of most fathers you know? Is it typical of most mothers? Is it typical of your father or your mother?
- In the story, it seems that the boy doesn't want to tell his father what he is thinking or feeling. Why do you think this is so? Is it because he fears or doesn't trust his father? Is it because he loves and respects him? Do you think the boy's behavior is typical of most children his age? Of girls as well as boys?
- If you were the boy's age, and sick, and thinking you were going to die, do you think you would behave the same way the boy behaved? Why, or why not?

## H. Writing: A Summary

In a summary, we present in a short form the important actions, facts, or meaning of a much longer piece of writing. Write a summary of "A Day's Wait" by answering the following questions with complete sentences and then placing your answers in a single paragraph. If there are underlined words in the questions, include them in your answers. The first two have been done for you.

- What sickness did <u>the boy in "A Day's Wait"</u> have?

  **The boy in "A Day's Wait" had influenza (or the flu).**

- What was <u>his temperature</u>?

  **His temperature was one hundred and two.**

- What did <u>the doctor</u> tell <u>the boy's father</u> about the boy's fever?
- <u>Alone with his father</u>, how did the boy act?
- Did the father think the boy was in danger or that he was just a little lightheaded?
- What did the father do <u>after giving the boy some prescribed capsules</u>?
- <u>While the father was away</u>, what did the boy refuse to do?
- Did he think his temperature was 102° Fahrenheit or 102° Celsius?
- What had he been waiting <u>all day</u> for?
- What did <u>his father</u> explain to him?
- Did the boy understand <u>his mistake</u>, or not?
- How did he behave the next day?

*3*

# APRIL SHOWERS

✺

### Adapted from the story by
### EDITH WHARTON

Edith Newbold Jones Wharton was born in New York City in 1862. Her family was wealthy—an "old" family of New York high society. Edith was taught at home by governesses. She learned French, read widely, and traveled in Europe at an early age. In 1885 she married Teddy Wharton, a young man from an upper-class Boston family. The marriage seemed a suitable one, but they were not happy. Teddy did not share Edith's interests in literature and the arts. Three years after their marriage, Edith suffered a nervous breakdown and was unwell for about six years. Finally, in 1913, they were divorced—an unusual, even shocking event at that time. By 1907 Wharton had moved to Paris and resumed the writing she had begun as a teenager. *The House of Mirth* (1905) was her first famous novel. This, like most of her writing, explores the false moral values of upper-class New York society, especially the lack of freedom for women. In 1921, she became the first woman to win the Pulitzer Prize for her novel *The Age of Innocence*. Wharton writes in a rather cool, formal style. She examines the weaknesses and failed efforts of her characters as if from a distance. There is little dialog. Yet the ironic humor with which she presents her characters' thoughts and feelings not only shows her understanding of the social pressures that trap them but also encourages us to feel sympathy with them. Wharton died in France in 1937. She had returned to the United States just once in all those years.

## BEFORE YOU READ THE STORY

### A. About the Author

Read the paragraph about Edith Wharton on page 29.  How was she educated when she was a girl?  Where did Wharton live for most of her adult life?  What kinds of people did Wharton usually write about?

### B. The Pictures

Look at the picture on page 36.  Where is the young woman standing?  What time of year is it?  What time of day?  What does she hold in her hand?  Describe the expression on her face.  How does she look?  Now look at the picture on page 39.  Where is the girl standing now?  How does she look now?

### C. Thinking About Dreams of Greatness

Many people dream of doing something great and becoming famous.  Sometimes these dreams come true; often they don't.  Have you ever had a dream of becoming famous?  What did you dream of doing?  Do you still dream of doing it? Are you afraid of failure?  Why, or why not?

### D. Skimming to Get an Impression

To get a general idea, or impression, of a piece of writing, we read it very quickly—that is, we skim it.  We don't try to find or understand details.

Skim paragraphs 1–12 of "April Showers."  Read only the first two or three sentences of each paragraph, and let your eyes move quickly over the rest of the text.  Then answer the following questions *without looking back at the paragraphs*.  Read for no more than three minutes. Check your answers after reading the entire story carefully.

1.  Someone named Theodora is obviously a character in this story.  How old do you think she is?
2.  Where does the action of the story seem to take place?
3.  An uncle named James is describing someone.  Is that person a businessman, a writer, or a housewife?
4.  What does Theodora seem to be most interested in?

"April Showers" includes several words related to the profession of writing. **Author** is a formal word for writer. A copy of an author's written work, called a **manuscript**, must be accepted by a **publisher**, the person or company that prepares it to be printed in a book or magazine. Usually, a written work must be **edited** before being published. Corrections and other changes are made by an **editor**. **Literature** is the general term used to include many types of well-written work. One type of writing, the **romance**, is a popular story of love or adventure of some kind. Because they are sometimes **sentimental**—emotional and unrealistic—romances are often considered a less valuable form of literature by **literary critics**, people whose job it is to judge and write about literature.

# APRIL SHOWERS

*B*ut Guy's heart slept under the violets on Muriel's
grave.

2     Theodora thought it was a beautiful ending. She had seen girls cry over last chapters that weren't half as sad as this one. She laid her pen aside and read the words again. Then, breathing deeply, she wrote across the bottom of the page the name she would use in literature—Gladys Glyn.

3     Downstairs the clock struck two. Two o'clock in the morning! And Theodora had promised her mother to be up early to sew buttons on Johnny's jacket, and to make sure that Kate and Bertha took their cod-liver oil[1] before school!

4     Slowly, tenderly, she gathered up the pages of her manuscript. There were five hundred of them. She tied them together with a blue satin ribbon. Her Aunt Julia had given the ribbon to her. She had wanted to wear it with her new white dress on Sunday. But this was a much nobler use for it. She tied the ends of the ribbon in a pretty bow. Theodora was clever at making bows. She could have been good at decorating things, but she gave all her spare time to literature. Then, with a last look at the precious pages, she

[1] cod-liver oil = an early source of vitamins, made from cod fish liver

closed and addressed the package. She would send it off next morning to *Home Circle*. She knew it would be hard to get published in this magazine, with all its popular authors. But she had been encouraged to try by her Uncle James.

5      Uncle James had been visiting from Boston, to tell them about his new house. "And who do you think is our new neighbor?" He smiled at Theodora. "Probably you know all about her. Ever hear of Kathleen Kyd?"

6      Kathleen Kyd! she thought with admiration. The famous novelist, author of more popular romances than all the other authors put together! The author of *Fashion and Passion, An American Duchess,* and *Rhona's Revolt*! Was there an intelligent girl from Maine to California whose heart would not beat faster at the sound of that name?

7      "Why, yes," Uncle James was saying. "Kathleen Kyd lives next door. Frances G. Wallop is her real name, and her husband's a dentist. She's a very pleasant kind of woman— you'd never know she was a writer. Ever hear how she began to write? She told me the whole story. It seems she was a saleswoman in a store, earning practically nothing. She had to support her mother and her sister, who's helplessly handicapped. Well, she wrote a story one day, just for fun, and sent it to *Home Circle*. They'd never heard of her, of course, and she never expected to hear from them. She did, though. They took her story and asked for more. She became a regular contributor. Now she tells me her books bring her in about ten thousand dollars[2] a year." He smiled ironically at Theodora's father. "That's rather more than you or I make, eh, John? I certainly hope *this* household doesn't contribute to her support." He looked sharply at Theodora. "I don't believe in feeding young people on sentimental romances!"

8      Theodora listened breathlessly. Kathleen Kyd's first story had been accepted by *Home Circle* and they had asked for more. Why should Gladys Glyn be less fortunate? Theodora had done a lot of romance reading—far more than her parents were aware of. She felt she could judge the quality of her own work. She was almost sure that her novel, *April Showers*, was a fine book. Perhaps it lacked Kathleen Kyd's tender humor. But it had an emotional

---

[2] ten thousand dollars = a very large amount of money at that time

depth that Kyd never reached. Theodora did not care to amuse her readers—she would leave that to less serious authors. Her aim was to stir the depths of human emotion,[3] and she felt she had succeeded. It was a great thing for a girl to feel that about her first novel. Theodora was only seventeen—she remembered with a touch of pity that the great author George Eliot[4] had not become famous until she was nearly forty.

9      No, there was no doubt that *April Showers* was a fine novel. But would a *less* fine book have a better chance to be published? Would it be wiser to write the book down to the average reader's level, and save for a future novel the great emotion that she had written into this book? No! Never would she change her words to suit ignorant taste! The great authors never sank to such tricks—nor would she. The manuscript should be sent as it was.

10     Theodora woke up suddenly, worried. What was it? *Home Circle* had refused *April Showers*? No, that couldn't be it. There lay the precious manuscript, waiting to be mailed. Ah, it was the clock downstairs, striking nine o'clock. It was Johnny's buttons, and the girls to get ready!

11     Theodora jumped out of bed feeling guilty. She didn't want to disappoint her mother about the buttons. Her mother was handicapped by rheumatism,[5] and had to give much of the care of the household to her oldest daughter. Theodora honestly meant to see that Johnny had all his buttons sewed back on, and that Kate and Bertha went to school tidy. Unfortunately, the writing of a great novel leaves little time or memory for the small responsibilities. Theodora usually found that her good intentions came too late for practical results.

12     Her guilt was softened by the thought that literary success would make up for all her little failings. She intended to spend all her money on her family. Already she could see the wheel chair she would buy for her mother, and the fresh wallpaper for her father's office. She would buy bicycles for the girls, and send Johnny to a boarding school where someone else would sew on his buttons. If her

---

[3] stir the depths of human emotion = cause to experience human emotions deeply
[4] George Eliot = a famous English novelist, Mary Ann Evans, who wrote using a man's name because she believed this would make her work more respected
[5] rheumatism = stiff, painful joints or muscles

parents could have guessed her intentions, they would not blame her for her failings. And her father, on this particular morning, would not have looked up to say, in his weary, ironic way,

13     "I suppose you didn't get home from the dance till morning?"

14     Theodora's sense of good intentions helped her take her father's criticism calmly.

15     "I'm sorry to be late, father," she said. Her tenderness would have quieted a parent in fiction, but Dr. Dace never behaved like a father in a book.

16     "Your apology shows your good manners," he said impatiently, "but manners won't keep your mother's breakfast warm."

17     "Hasn't mother's tray gone up yet?"

18     "Who was to take it, I'd like to know? The girls came down so late that I had to hurry them off before they'd finished breakfast. And Johnny's hands were so dirty that I sent him back to his room to clean up. It's a fine thing when the doctor's children are the dirtiest children in town!"

19     Theodora quickly prepared her mother's tray, leaving her own breakfast untouched. As she entered the room upstairs her mother smiled tenderly at her. But Mrs. Dace's patience was harder to bear than Dr. Dace's criticism.

20     "Mother, I'm *so* sorry—"

21     "No matter, dear. I suppose Johnny's buttons kept you. I can't think what that boy does to his clothes!"

22     Theodora set the tray down without answering. She couldn't talk about her forgetfulness without giving away the cause of it. For a few weeks longer she would have to be misunderstood. Then—ah, then, if her novel was accepted, how gladly she would forget and forgive misunderstanding! But what if it were refused? She turned away from her mother to hide her worry. Well, if it was refused, she would ask her parents to forgive *her*. She would settle down without complaining to a wasted life of sewing and cod-liver oil.

23     Theodora had said to herself that after the manuscript had been sent off, she would have time to look after the children. But she hadn't thought about the mailman. He came three times a day. For an hour before each visit, she

was too excited to work, wondering if he would bring an answer this time. And for an hour after he left she moved about in a heavy cloud of disappointment. Meanwhile, the children had never been so difficult. They seemed always to be coming to pieces like cheap furniture. Mrs. Dace worried herself ill over Johnny's clothes, Bertha's bad marks at school, and Kate's refusal to take her cod-liver oil. And Dr. Dace came home late from visiting his patients to find a cold fireplace and nothing to eat. He called angrily for Theodora to come downstairs and take the embroidered[6] words, "East, West, Home is Best" down off the wall.

24    The week was a long nightmare. Theodora could neither eat nor sleep. She was up early enough. But instead of taking care of the children and making breakfast, she wandered down the street to meet the mailman. Then she would come back empty-handed, forgetting her morning responsibilities. She had no idea how long she would be forced to wait, but she didn't see how authors could live if they were kept waiting more than a week.

25    Then, suddenly, one evening—she never knew how or when it happened—she found herself with a *Home Circle* envelope in her hand. Her eyes flashed over the letter—a wild dance of words that wouldn't settle down and make sense.

26    "Dear Madam:" (They called her Madam!) And then, yes, the words were beginning to fall into line now. "Your novel, *April Showers*, has been received, and we are glad to accept it on the usual terms. Chapters of a novel we were planning to start publishing were delayed due to the author's illness. The first chapter of *April Showers* will therefore appear in our midsummer edition. Thanking you for sending this contribution, Sincerely yours . . ." and so forth.

27    Theodora ran outside into the spring evening. Spring! Everything was crowding toward the light, and in her own heart, hundreds of hopes burst into leaf. She looked up through the trees at the tender moon. She felt surrounded by an atmosphere of loving understanding. The brown earth was full of joy. The treetops moved with joy. A joyous star burst through the branches, as if to say, "I know!"

---

[6] embroidered = sewn with decorative colored thread

28     Theodora, on the whole, behaved very well.  Her mother cried, her father whistled, and said (but less ironically than usual) that he supposed he'd never get a hot meal again.  And the children added noisily to this unfamiliar, joyous scene.

29     Within a week, everybody in town knew that Theodora had written a novel, and that it was coming out in *Home Circle*.  Other girls copied her way of dressing and speaking.  The local newspaper asked her for a poem.  Her old school teachers stopped to shake her hand, and shyly congratulated her.  Uncle James even came down from Boston to talk about her success.  From what Kathleen Kyd told him, he thought Theodora would probably get a thousand dollars for her story.  He suggested that she should give him the money to buy shares in a company he was interested in, and suggested a plot for her next romance.

30     Theodora waited impatiently for the midsummer *Home Circle*—and at last the great day came.  Before the book store opened, Theodora was waiting on the sidewalk to buy the midsummer *Home Circle*.  She ran home without opening the precious magazine.  Her excitement was almost more than she could bear.  Not hearing her father call her to breakfast, she ran upstairs and locked herself in her room.  Her hands shook so that she could hardly turn the pages.  At last—yes, there it was: *April Showers*.

31     The magazine dropped from her hands.  What name had she read beneath the title?  Had her emotion blinded her?

32     "*April Showers*, by Kathleen Kyd"

33     Kathleen Kyd! Oh, cruel misprint! Oh, careless editor!  Through tears of furious disappointment, Theodora looked again.  Yes, she had made no mistake—it was that hateful name.  She found herself reading a paragraph that she had never seen before.  She read farther.  It was all strange.  The truth burst upon her: *it was not her story!*

34     It was hours later.  Theodora never knew how she had got back to the Boston train station.  She had struggled through the crowd, and was pushed into the train.  It would be dark when she got home, but that didn't matter.  Nothing mattered now.  She sank into her seat, and closed her eyes.  She tried to shut out what had happened in the

last few hours, but minute by minute her memory forced her to relive the experience.

35    Although she didn't know Boston well, she had made her way easily enough to the *Home Circle* building. At least, she supposed she had. She remembered nothing until she found herself going up the stairs as easily as one does unbelievable things in dreams. She must have been walking fast, for her heart was beating furiously. She barely had breath to whisper the editor's name to the young man who met her. He led her to an inner office which seemed filled by a huge force. Theodora felt herself overpowered, conquered by this force—she could hardly speak or hear.

36    Gradually, words floated up around her. "*April Showers*, Mrs. Kyd's new novel? *Your* manuscript, you say? You have a letter from me? The name, please? It must be some unfortunate misunderstanding. One moment." And then a bell was ringing, the young man was unlocking a cupboard, and the manuscript, her own precious manuscript, tied with Aunt Julia's ribbon, was laid on the table before her. Her stream of angry questions was drowned in a flood of pleasant apology: "An unfortunate accident—Mrs. Kyd's manuscript received the same day—how strange you chose the same title—two acceptance letters sent by mistake—Miss Dace's novel didn't suit their needs—should, of course, have been returned—so sorry—accidents would happen—sure she understood—."

37    The voice went on. When it stopped, Theodora found herself in the street. A taxi nearly ran her over. A car honked in her ears. She held her manuscript tenderly in the crowd, like a live thing that had been hurt. She could not bear to look at its soiled edges, and the ink spot on Aunt Julia's ribbon.

38    The train stopped suddenly. It was her stop. She saw other passengers getting off and she followed them into the darkness. A warm wind blew into her face the smell of summer woods. She thought back to the spring when she had been so full of joy. Then she thought of home. She had run out in the morning without a word. Her heart sank at the thought of her mother's fears. And her father—how angry he would be! She bent her head under the coming storm of his criticism.

39    The night was cloudy, and as she stepped into the darkness a hand was slipped into hers. She stood still, too weary to feel frightened. A voice said, quietly:

40    "Don't walk so fast, child. You look tired."

41    "Father! You were at the station?" she whispered.

42    "It's such a good night, I thought I'd wander down and meet you."

43    She could not see his face in the darkness, but the light of his cigar looked down on her like a friendly eye. She took courage to say, "Then you knew—"

44    "That you'd gone to Boston? Well, I thought you probably had."

45    They walked on slowly, and then he added, "You see, you left the *Home Circle* lying in your room."

46    How she blessed the dark sky! She couldn't have borne even the tiniest star to look at her. "Then Mother wasn't much frightened?"

47    "Why, no, she didn't seem to be. She's been busy all day over some sewing for Bertha."

48    Theodora's voice was choked with tears. "Father, I'll—" She reached for words, but they escaped her. "I'll do things —differently; I haven't meant—" Suddenly she heard herself bursting out: "It was all a mistake, you know—about my story. They didn't want it; they won't have it!" She couldn't bear his amusement.

49    She felt his arm around her, and was sure he was laughing. But they moved on in silence. Then he said:

50    "It hurts a bit just at first, doesn't it?"

51    "Oh, Father!"

52    He stood still a moment, and the light of his cigar shone on his face. "You see, I've been through it myself."

53    "You, Father? You?"

54    "Why, yes. Didn't I ever tell you? I wrote a novel once. I was just out of college, and didn't want to be a doctor. No; I wanted to be a brilliant writer. So I wrote a novel."

55    The doctor paused, and Theodora held fast to his arm in silent sympathy. It was as if a drowning creature caught a live hand in the murderous fury of the waves.

56    "It took me a year—a whole year's hard work. When I'd finished, no publisher would have it, not at any price. That's why I came to meet you, because I remembered my walk home."

# AFTER YOU READ THE STORY

## A. Understanding the Plot

Answer the following questions with complete sentences.

1. Who, or what, is Gladys Glyn?
2. Who is Kathleen Kyd? What is her real name?
3. What has Theodora written? What is its title? Where does she send her manuscript?
4. What kinds of household jobs do Theodora's parents expect her to do?
5. How do Theodora's family, teachers, and others behave toward her when they hear that her book has been accepted?
6. What does Theodora discover when she reads the midsummer *Home Circle*? Where does she go?
7. When she gets there, what does she find out?
8. Who meets Theodora at the train station? Why?

## B. Understanding Words in Context

Look at the underlined word or phrase in the quotations from the story. After considering the context, circle the choice that best defines the underlined word or phrase. Paragraph numbers are given to help you find more context for the underlined words. Check your answers with a partner.

**Example:** *But Guy's heart slept under the <u>violets</u> on Muriel's grave. (1)*

    **a.** stones  **(b.)** flowers  **c.** blankets

1. *Edith was taught at home by <u>governesses</u>.* (biographical paragraph, p. 29)

    **a.** government textbooks  **b.** private teachers  **c.** parents

2. *She tied them together with a blue <u>satin</u> ribbon.* (4)

    **a.** smooth, shiny material  **b.** string  **c.** rough, heavy material

3. *Would a less fine book have a better chance to be published? Would it be wiser to <u>write</u> the book <u>down</u> to the average reader's level?* (9)

    **a.** write by hand    **b.** type    **c.** simplify

**4.** *Her guilt was softened by the thought that literary success would __make up for__ all her little failings.* (12)

    **a.** explain           **b.** create           **c.** excuse

**5.** *[Uncle James] suggested . . . a __plot__ for her next romance.* (29)

    **a.** place           **b.** action of a story   **c.** secret plan

**6.** *She had __struggled__ through the crowd, and was pushed into the train.* (34)

    **a.** forced her way      **b.** wandered        **c.** become lost

## C. Close Reading: Irony and Inference

The paragraph about Edith Wharton on page 29 tells us that she often presents her characters with "ironic humor." Irony is a tone (of voice or writing) used to express the opposite of what the speaker or writer means, usually in a humorous way. It sometimes requires the reader to *infer* (or conclude) that what an author writes or a character says is different from what he or she really means. Below are some examples of this type of humor from the story. Read them closely and answer the questions that follow.

**1.** When Theodora comes to breakfast late, her father says, *"I suppose you didn't get home from the dance till morning?"* (13)

Does Dr. Dace really think Theodora went dancing the night before? What do we infer from his reaction to her lateness? What does he really mean?

**2.** After she finishes her book, Theodora imagines she has written a deeply moving story. *It was a great thing for a girl to feel that about her first novel. Theodora was only seventeen—she remembered with a touch of pity that the great author George Eliot had not become famous until she was nearly forty.* (8)

Why does Theodora "pity" a great novelist? Does the author want us to infer that Theodora has written an equally fine book herself?

3. *And Dr. Dace came home late from visiting his patients to find a cold fireplace and nothing to eat. He called angrily for Theodora to come downstairs and take the embroidered words, "East, West, Home is Best" down off the wall.* (23)

   Does Dr. Dace really want Theodora to take down the embroidered saying? What is he really trying to tell her?

4. After Theodora tells her parents that her novel has been accepted, *Her mother cried, her father whistled, and said (but less ironically than usual) that he supposed he'd never get a hot meal again.* (28)

   What does Dr. Dace mean when he says this? What can we infer about his real feelings?

## D. Vocabulary Practice

Complete the sentences below in a way that shows you understand the meaning of the underlined word. Paragraph numbers show where the word first appears in the story. The first one has been done for you.

1. Theodora gathered up the pages of her book <u>tenderly</u> because **she felt lovingly protective of her work**. (4)

2. Because they were <u>handicapped</u>, both Theodora's mother and Kathleen Kyd's sister _____ _____. (7)

3. Uncle James thinks that <u>sentimental</u> romances are _____ _____. (7)

4. Although Theodora thought that the average reader was <u>ignorant</u>, she decided not to _____ _____. (9)

5. To please her mother and father, Theodora's <u>intention</u> was to _____. (11)

## E. Word Forms

| Noun | Verb | Adjective | Adverb |
|------|------|-----------|--------|
| apology | apologize | apologetic | apologetically |
| complaint | complain | complaining | complainingly |
| congratulation(s) | congratulate | congratulatory | |
| contribution, contributor | contribute | contributing | |
| criticism, critic | criticize | critical | critically |
| intent, intention | intend | intentional | intentionally |

Using the chart above, chose the correct forms of the word to complete the following sentences. Be sure to add the correct verb endings when necessary.

1. *(contribute)* Theodora hopes to become a regular

   _____ to *Home Circle* when she sends in her

   first _____.

2. *(criticize)* Dr. Dace is _____ of Theodora's

   behavior, but she tries to be patient with his _____.

3. *(intend)* Theodora is not _____ forgetful of her

   brother and sisters. She _____ to do better after

   her book is accepted.

4. *(congratulate)* Theodora is excited to receive the

   _____ letter from *Home Circle*. Her parents, and

   even her teachers, offer her their _____ when they

   hear her novel has been accepted.

5. *(complain)* Theodora promises herself that she will not

   _____ about helping with the little children if her

   novel is refused, but she does go to the *Home Circle* editor

   to express her _____ about the mistake she thinks

   the magazine must have made.

6. *(apologize)* The editor of *Home Circle* _____ to Theodora for mixing up her story with Kathleen Kyd's. But Theodora thinks her _____ is weak.

## F. Discussion: Your Opinion

1. What do you think of Theodora's father, Dr. Dace? Why is he critical of Theodora? What does he expect of Theodora, and why? Are his expectations fair? Why, or why not? Were you surprised by his behavior at the end of the story? Why, or why not?

2. What do you think of Theodora? Did you like her and feel sympathy for her? Or did you think she was silly to believe she could be a famous writer? Do you know a young person who had a dream and then, like Theodora, actually worked hard to try to achieve it? Do you think young people should work toward achieving their dreams of glory even when they are quite young? Why, or why not?

## G. Language Activity: An Improvisation

An improvisation is a short play or scene that the actors make up as they go along. Work with a partner or small group if possible, and choose one of the situations below to act out in front of the class. Decide together how you want your scene to develop, based on what you know of the characters. Try to speak naturally and to express what the character would think and feel. Possible first lines are suggested to get you started, but feel free to make up your own first lines, if you prefer.

1. Uncle James and Dr. Dace are discussing the author, Kathleen Kyd. Dr. Dace has not heard of her, and James tells him about her writing. What does he think of her? How does Dr. Dace respond?

   Possible first lines: James: You'll never guess who lives next door to our new house.
   Dace: Who is it?

2. Dr. Dace is trying to get the three younger children to eat breakfast and get ready for school.

Possible first lines: Dace: Come on, children, it's time for breakfast!

Kate: What's for breakfast? I'm hungry!

Johnny: Where's Theodora? I can't find my jacket!

Bertha: Kate, where is my homework? I left it right on the table . . .

3. Theodora has overslept, and brings the breakfast tray late to her mother. What do they say to each other?

Possible first lines: Theodora: Mother, I'm *so* sorry . . .

Mother: No matter, dear. I suppose Johnny's buttons kept you.

4. Theodora is on her way to the book store to buy the new *Home Circle* with her story in it. On the way, she meets her old English teacher, who has heard that she has had a story accepted.

Possible first lines: Teacher: Good morning, Theodora! I miss you in class this year. Where are you going, so early?

Theodora: Well, I'm going to the book store . . .

5. Theodora has gone to the editor of *Home Circle* to find out why her story is not in the magazine.

Possible first lines: Editor: Good afternoon, Miss er, ah, Miss Dace, is it?

Theodora: Yes, my name is Theodora Dace.

## H. Writing: A Romance

Although a romance is often a love story, it can also include adventure, drama, and humor. Write the beginning three paragraphs (about 150 words) of a story (novel or short story) using one of Kathleen Kyd's titles: *Fashion and Passion, An American Duchess,* or *Rhona's Revolt.* Or make up your own title, and write the first three paragraphs of a romance from your own imagination.

*4*

# RIP VAN WINKLE

✳

Adapted from the story by
**WASHINGTON IRVING**

Washington Irving was the first person born in America to succeed as a professional writer. He was the first widely read American writer of short stories and became the first American to win recognition in Europe for his literary work. Irving was born in 1783 in New York City, the youngest of eleven children. His wealthy parents named him for General George Washington, who led the American army during the Revolutionary War (1775–1781) and later became the first president of the United States. Irving was a lively child who was so bored by school that after the age of sixteen he stopped formal studies. He published his first humorous writing when he was nineteen, traveled in Europe, read widely, and educated himself in that way. In 1809 he published *A History of New York, by Dietrich Knickerbocker,* a humorous book that had great success. Irving was not yet ready for a literary career, however, and he joined his brother's business, exporting household goods. In 1815 he went to live in Europe to represent the family company. When the business failed, he started writing seriously for a living. In 1819, while he was living in England, he published *A Sketch Book*, which includes two famous stories, "The Legend of Sleepy Hollow" and "Rip Van Winkle." He returned to Europe frequently during his long life, and for three years he was the American ambassador to Spain. One of Irving's last works was *The Life of Washington,* which he considered his finest book. Soon after completing it, he died at Sunnyside—his home on the Hudson River in New York State—in 1859.

# BEFORE YOU READ THE STORY

## A. About the Author

Read the paragraph about Washington Irving on page 47. Where did the name "Washington" come from? In addition to his work as a writer, what other professions did Irving pursue during his life?

## B. The Pictures

In the picture on page 54, the men are playing a game called **nine-pins**. What seems strange about their clothing? The man carrying a gun in this picture appears again in the picture on page 58. What changes do you see in him?

## C. Thinking About Revolution

Irving's story takes place both before and after the American Revolutionary War. By winning this war, which lasted from 1775 to 1781, the United States gained its freedom from England. During such **revolutions**, one government is violently removed and another put in its place. Other famous revolutions include the French Revolution (1789), when the French people rose up against the French king and nobles, and the Russian Revolution (1917), when Russian soldiers and workers fought against the tsar and his ministers. From what you know of these or other political revolutions, do you think revolutions happen because they must happen or because a few strong people make them happen? Do you think that life for ordinary people after a revolution is likely easier or more difficult than before? Why?

## D. Skimming to Get an Impression

Skim paragraphs 1–11 of "Rip Van Winkle" by reading the first sentence or two of each paragraph. Take no more than three minutes to do this. Then answer as many of the following questions as you can. Write down your answers. Then check them after you have read the story carefully.
1. Does this story occur in a city, a town, or a country village?
2. What word or words might you use to describe Rip's character?

3. What word or words might you use to describe Rip's marriage?
4. Where does Rip walk one day?
5. What strange people does he meet?

## KEY WORDS

In "Rip Van Winkle," we are presented with a **shrewish** wife and a **henpecked** husband (a **shrew** is a small, fierce field mouse; a hen is a female chicken who **pecks** at corn, seed, and sometimes the heads of other chickens). The shrewish woman spends a lot of time complaining to her husband about what he does or doesn't do; and the henpecked husband spends a lot of time avoiding his wife. In Irving's story, the henpecked man is Rip Van Winkle; his wife is called **Dame**, an old word for "Mrs." The story takes place in what is now New York State, a region that was originally settled by the **Dutch** (the people of The Netherlands, or Holland) and later became a **colony**, or political possession, of Great Britain (England).

# RIP VAN WINKLE

Whoever has made a voyage up the Hudson River must remember the Catskill mountains. They are seen away to the west of the river, rising up to a noble height. Every change of season, every change of weather, indeed every hour of the day, produces some change in their magical colors and shapes.

2    At the foot of these mountains the voyager may have noticed the light smoke curving upwards from a village set among the trees. It is a little village of great age. It was built by Dutch colonists in early times. The houses were made of small yellow bricks brought from Holland, and they were built in the old style of Dutch country houses.

3    In that same village, and in one of those very houses (which to tell the exact truth was sadly time-worn and weather-beaten), there lived a simple good-natured fellow named Rip Van Winkle. This was many years ago, when

the country was still a colony of Great Britain. Even before that, the Van Winkle family had served bravely in the army of the Dutch Governor, Peter Stuyvesant. Rip, however, was not blessed with his family's war-like character. I have said that he was a simple good-natured fellow; he was moreover a kind neighbor and an obedient, henpecked husband. Indeed, the mildness of spirit that made him so popular in his village may have come from being so henpecked in his house. After all, consider the men who are sweet, easy, and willing to please in the world; they are often those who are under the control of a sharp-tongued shrew at home. By causing this sweetness in her husband, a shrewish wife may in some ways be considered a reasonable blessing—and if so, Rip Van Winkle was thoroughly blessed.

4      It is certain that he was a great favorite among all the good wives of the village. They always took his side in family quarrels and lay all the blame on Dame Van Winkle. The children of the village, too, would shout with joy whenever he approached. He taught them games, made their playthings, and told them long stories of ghosts and devils and Indians. The children followed him all over the village, hanging on his coat and playing tricks on him. And not a dog would bark at him throughout the village.

5      The great weakness in Rip's character was a powerful dislike of all kinds of profitable work. This laziness could not be from a lack of patience or energy. He could sit on a wet rock and fish all day without a single complaint. He could carry a heavy gun on his shoulder for hours, walking through woods and up hills, to shoot a few rabbits or wild birds. He would never refuse to help a neighbor with the roughest work. And he was the best man for preparing Indian corn at all country parties, or for building stone fences, or for doing little jobs for the women of the village that their husbands wouldn't do. In a word, Rip was ready to pay attention to anybody's business but his own. To do his family duty or to keep his farm in order—he found these things impossible. His own poor farm—the falling-down fences, the wandering cow, the bare field—was the worst in the village. His son and daughter were poorly dressed and wild. They, and Rip's dog, Wolf, looked like they belonged to nobody.

6      Rip Van Winkle, however, was one of those happy men

of foolish, easygoing natures who take the world lightly, eat white bread or brown, and would rather go hungry on a penny than work for a dollar.  Alone, Rip would have whistled life away in perfect happiness.  But his wife kept shouting in his ears about his laziness, his carelessness, and the ruin he was bringing on his family.  Morning, noon, and night, her tongue was going non-stop.  Everything Rip did produced a flood of shrewish talk.  Rip's only reply to these angry speeches was to lift his shoulders, shake his head, roll his eyes, and go outside of the house—the only side which, in truth, belongs to the henpecked husband.

7    Times grew worse and worse with Rip Van Winkle as the years of marriage went by; a bitter heart never sweetens with age, and a tongue is the only edged tool that grows sharper with frequent use.  Forced from home, Rip often found pleasure in a kind of club of wise men, philosophers, and other non-working men of the village.  They held their meetings under a great tree in front of the village inn, which travelers knew by its sign, a painted picture of King George the Third of England.  Here the club's members used to sit in the shade through a long, lazy summer's day, talking of village matters, or telling endless, sleepy stories about nothing.  Derrick Van Bummel, the well-dressed little schoolmaster, would sometimes read to them from an old newspaper.  They would discuss with great seriousness events that had taken place some months before.  These discussions were guided by the innkeeper, Nicholas Vedder, and his pipe. He never spoke a word, but when he disagreed with an opinion, black smoke came in quantity from the pipe, and when he agreed, he removed the pipe from his mouth and let the smoke curl sweetly about his nose.

8    Even from this favorite hiding place, however, Rip was chased by his wife.  She would break in on the peaceful club meetings and direct her anger at all the club's members for encouraging laziness in her husband.  In the end, poor Rip found only one way to escape the labor of the farm and the anger of Dame Van Winkle.  This was to take gun in hand and walk away into the woods.  He would sometimes sit at the foot of a tree and share his simple meal with Wolf, whom he saw as a fellow-sufferer.  "Poor Wolf," he would say, "your lady leads you a dog's life; but never mind, my boy, while I live you will never lack a friend to stand by

you!" The dog would wag his tail and look sadly in his master's face; and if dogs can feel pity, I do believe he returned the feeling with all his heart.

9      On one of these wanderings on a fine autumn day, Rip had unknowingly climbed to one of the highest parts of the Catskill mountains. He was hunting rabbits, and the stillness of the woodlands had echoed and re-echoed with the sound of his gun. Tired and out of breath, he threw himself, late in the afternoon, on a small round green hill covered with mountain bushes. From an opening between the trees he could overlook all the lower country with its miles of rich woodland. He saw at a distance the lordly Hudson River, far, far below him, moving on its silent but noble course. On the other side he looked down into a deep mountain valley, wild and lonely, the bottom filled with rocks that had fallen from the high hills above. Evening was approaching. The mountains began to throw their long blue shadows over the valleys. He saw that it would be dark before he could reach the village, and he sighed heavily when he thought of being met with the terrors of Dame Van Winkle.

10      As he was about to descend, he heard a voice from a distance, shouting, "Rip Van Winkle! Rip Van Winkle!" He looked round, but could see nothing but a blackbird flying its lonely way across the mountain. He thought his imagination must have tricked him, and turned again to descend, when he heard the same cry through the still evening air: "Rip Van Winkle! Rip Van Winkle!" Wolf made a low noise in his throat and drew nearer to his master's side, looking fearfully down the valley. Rip now felt a strong uncertainty coming over him. He looked anxiously in the same direction, and saw a strange figure working its way up the rocks, and bending under the weight of something he carried on his back. Rip was surprised to see any human being in this lonely place, but thinking it might be one of the villagers in need of his help, he hurried down to give it.

11      As he approached he was still more surprised by the stranger's appearance. He was a short square-built old fellow, with thick bushy hair and a beard. He was dressed in the old Dutch fashion—a short cloth coat belted at the waist, and broad trousers gathered at the knees. He carried

on his back a heavy barrel, the kind that holds beer or whiskey, and he made signs for Rip to approach and help with his load. Though rather shy and distrustful of the stranger, Rip gave help with his usual speed. Helping each other, they climbed up the dry bed of a mountain stream. As they climbed, Rip heard long, deep rolling sounds, like distant thunder. The sound seemed to come out of an opening in the hill above them. He stopped briefly, but decided that it was only a mountain thunder-shower, and continued to climb. Passing through the opening in the hill, the two men came into a round open space, an amphitheater. It was surrounded by high hills with tall trees on their tops, so you could see little of the darkening sky or the bright evening cloud. During the whole time Rip and the stranger had climbed in silence. Although Rip wondered greatly at the purpose of carrying a barrel of strong drink up this wild mountain, there was something strange about the unknown that kept him silent.

12     On entering the amphitheater, he was greeted by still more unusual sights. On a level spot in the center was a company of odd-looking fellows playing at nine-pins, slowly rolling the balls at the wooden pins. Some of the men wore jackets, others wore short coats, with knives in their belts. Most of them wore broad trousers like Rip's guide. Their whole appearance was strange. One had a large head, broad face, and small piggish eyes. Another's face seemed to consist mostly of nose, and was topped by a pointed white hat with a red feather in it. There was one who seemed to be the commander. He was a fat old gentleman, with a weather-beaten face. He wore a formal black jacket, a broad belt and sword, red stockings, and high-heeled shoes with roses on them. The whole group reminded Rip of the figures in an old Dutch painting he had seen in the house of Dominic Van Shaick, the village minister, and which had been brought over from Holland when the colony was first settled.

13     What seemed especially odd to Rip was the way these folks played at their game of nine-pins. They kept the most serious faces as they played, and the most mysterious silence. The only sound was that of the balls hitting the wooden pins and echoing along the mountains like rolling thunder.

14    As Rip and his companion approached them, they suddenly stopped their play. They looked straight at him with such statue-like faces that his heart turned within him, and his knees knocked together. His companion now emptied the contents of the barrel into large drinking cups, and made signs for him to serve the company. He obeyed, shaking with fear. The men drank in the deepest silence, and then returned to their game.

15    Gradually, Rip's anxiety lessened. He even dared, when no eye was fixed upon him, to taste the drink, which he thought had much the flavor of a fine Holland whiskey. He was naturally a thirsty fellow, and soon allowed himself a second drink. One taste led to another, and he repeated his visits to the drinking cup so often that finally his senses were overpowered. His eyes swam in his head, his head gradually dropped to his chest, and he fell into a deep sleep.

16    When he awoke, he found himself on the small round green hill where he had first seen his companion, the old man of the valley. He rubbed his eyes—it was a bright sunny morning. The birds were jumping and singing in the bushes. "Surely," thought Rip, "I have not slept here all night?" He remembered what had happened before he fell asleep. The strange man with the barrel—the climb up the dry stream-bed—the amphitheater among the rocks—the strange serious party at nine-pins—the drinking cup. "Oh! That cup! That evil cup!" thought Rip. "What excuse shall I make to Dame Van Winkle?"

17    He looked round for his gun, but in place of the clean well-oiled weapon, he found an old gun, its iron time-worn and its wood worm-eaten. He now suspected that the serious games-players of the mountain had tricked him with strong drink and stolen his gun. Wolf, too, had disappeared, though he might have gone after rabbits or birds. He whistled for him and called his name, but no dog came.

18    He decided to revisit the scene of last night's events, and if he met with any of the group, to demand his gun and his dog. As he rose to walk, he felt an unusual tightness in his legs, arms, and all his body. "These mountain beds do not agree with me," thought Rip. He descended again into the deep valley. He found the dry stream-bed which he and his

companion had climbed up the evening before. But to his great surprise a mountain stream was now rushing down it, leaping from rock to rock and filling the valley with its pleasant sound. With difficulty he climbed up its sides, fighting his way through thick bushes and the branches of small trees.

19     Finally, he came to the place where an opening had led through the hill to the amphitheater; but no signs of such an opening remained. Only high rocks greeted him, and the stream that flowed quickly over them. Here, then, poor Rip was brought to a stop. He called again and whistled for his dog; he was answered only by the blackbirds flying high in the trees above him. What could he do? The morning was passing away, and he was very hungry. He shook his head, shouldered the old gun, and turned his steps toward home.

20     As he approached the village, he met a number of people, but he knew none of them. This surprised him, for he had thought he knew everyone in the country around. Their clothes, too, were in a fashion different from the one he knew. They looked equally surprised to meet him. Many of them brought their hands to their chins when they saw him, and when Rip copied the movement he found, to his surprise, that his beard had grown a foot long!

21     He had now entered the village. A group of strange children ran at his heels, shouting after him and pointing at his long gray beard. The dogs barked as he passed. The village itself was changed; it was larger, with many more people. There were rows of houses he had never seen before. Strange names were over the doors—strange faces at the windows—everything was strange. He began to wonder whether some kind of magic was at work. Surely this was his own village, which he had left just the day before. There stood the Catskill mountains; there was the silver Hudson at a distance. Rip was very confused. "That cup last night," thought he, "has mixed up my brain thoroughly!"

22     It was with some difficulty that he found the way to his own house, which he approached with some fear, expecting every moment to hear the angry voice of Dame Van Winkle. But he found the house in ruins—the roof fallen in, the windows broken, the doors hanging off. He entered the house, which, to tell the truth, Dame Van Winkle had

always kept in neat order. It was a sad, empty shell. Frightened, he called loudly for his wife and children. The lonely rooms rang for a moment with his voice, and then all again was silence.

23    He now hurried away toward his club's old meeting place at the village's small inn—but it too was gone. In its place stood a large ugly wooden building with the word HOTEL above the door. Instead of the great tree in front of it, there was a tall wooden pole, and from it hung a flag with a strange pattern of stars and stripes in red, white, and blue. He saw the inn's old sign, but even this was changed. King George's round face was the same, but his red coat was changed to one of blue. Instead of a crown, he wore a hat and held a sword. And underneath the picture, in large letters, was painted: GENERAL WASHINGTON.

24    There was, as usual, a crowd of folk near the door, but no one that Rip remembered. He looked for wise old Nicholas Vedder with his pipe, or the little schoolmaster Van Bummel, reading from an old newspaper. In place of these men, a thin, nervous-looking fellow was shouting a speech to the crowd about government—freedom—citizens—elections—heroes of the revolutionary war—and other words completely unknown to the confused Van Winkle.

25    The appearance of Rip, with his long beard, old gun, strange clothes, and an army of women and children at his heels, attracted the attention of the politicians in the crowd. They gathered round him, eyeing him from head to foot with great curiosity. The thin speech-maker hurried up to him, and bringing him to one side, asked "on which side he voted?" Rip looked at him with complete, empty stupidity. "I say, which political party do you belong to?" the man insisted. Rip had no idea how to answer such a question. Then a knowing, self-important gentleman made his way through the crowd, putting folks to the right and left with his elbows as he passed. He positioned himself before Van Winkle, and demanded in a serious voice "what brought him to the election with a gun on his shoulder and a wild crowd at his heels, and whether he meant to cause trouble in the village?"—"Oh, dear, gentlemen," cried Rip, "I am a poor quiet man, a native of the place, and a faithful subject of the king, God bless him!"

26      Here a general shout burst from the bystanders: "A spy! a spy! the enemy! away with him!" It was with great difficulty that the self-important man brought order again to the crowd. Then, with even deeper seriousness than before, he demanded of the stranger why he had come there, and whom he was searching for? The poor man promised that he meant no harm, but merely came in search of some of his neighbors, who used to meet at the old hotel.

27      "Well—who are they?—name them."

28      Rip thought for a moment, then asked, "Where's Nicholas Vedder?"

29      There was a silence for a while, then an old man replied, in a thin little voice, "Nicholas Vedder! Why, he is dead and gone these eighteen years! There was a wooden marker in the churchyard that used to tell about him, but that's rotten and gone, too."

30      "Where's Van Bummel, the schoolmaster?"

31      "Oh, he went off to the army, right at the beginning of the war. He became a famous general, and now he's in the government."

32      Rip's heart died away at hearing of these sad changes in his home and friends, and finding himself so alone in the world. Every answer puzzled him, too, by mentioning matters he could not understand—eighteen years, and war, and revolution, and government. So when the self-important man finally asked him who he was, he cried out, "God knows! I'm not myself—I'm somebody else—I was myself last night, but I fell asleep on the mountain, and they've changed my gun, and everything's changed, and I'm changed, and I can't tell what's my name or who I am!"

33      The by-standers began now to look at each other, give little smiles, close one eye, and press their fingers against their foreheads. At this very moment, a pretty young woman passed through the crowd to have a look at the gray-bearded man. She had a round little child in her arms who, frightened by the strange old man, began to cry. "Hush, Rip," cried she, "hush, you little fool; the old man won't hurt you." The name of the child, the look of the mother, something in her voice, all awakened memories in his mind. "What is your name, my good woman?" asked he.

34    "Judith Gardenier."

35    "And your father's name?"

36    "Ah, poor man, Rip Van Winkle was his name, but it's twenty years since he went away from home with his gun, and never has been heard of since. His dog came home without him; but whether he shot himself or was carried away by Indians, nobody can tell. I was only a little girl then."

37    Rip had only one more question to ask; but he said with a shaking voice: "Where's your mother?"

38    "Oh, she too died, just a short time ago. She had a heart attack while shouting at a traveling salesman."

39    There was some comfort, at least, in this information. The honest man could no longer control himself. He gathered his daughter and her child in his arms. "I am your father!" he cried. "Young Rip Van Winkle once; old Rip Van Winkle now! Does nobody know poor Rip Van Winkle?"

40    All stood in silent wonder, until an old woman came out of the crowd, looked closely at his face for a moment, and finally cried, "Sure enough! It is Rip Van Winkle! It is himself! Welcome home again, old neighbor. Why, where have you been these twenty long years?!"

41    Rip's story was soon told, for the entire twenty years had been to him just as one night. The neighbors at first could not believe it. They shook their heads in doubt, and smiled their smiles at each other. However, they decided to get the opinion of old Peter Vanderdonk, who was seen then slowly advancing up the road. He was descended from the famous historian of that name, who wrote one of the earliest accounts of the region. Peter was the oldest man in the village, and very knowledgeable about all the wonderful events and traditions of the neighborhood. He remembered Rip immediately, and supported his story in the most satisfactory manner. He stated as a historical fact that the Catskill mountains had always had magical qualities. There was no doubt, he said, that the great Hendrick Hudson, the first discoverer of the river and country, returned every twenty years with the crew of his ship. In this way, Hudson could revisit the scene of his adventures and keep a guardian

eye on the river. Vanderdonk's own father had once seen them in their old Dutch clothes playing at nine-pins in a valley of the mountains. And he himself had heard, one summer afternoon, the sound of their balls, like distant rolling thunder.

42    To make a long story short, the company broke up, and returned to the more important matters of the election. Rip's daughter took him home to live with her. And in time, Rip again began his old walks and habits. He soon found many of his old friends, all of them rather the worse for the wear and tear of time. He preferred the younger people of the village, who grew to like him, too. He could often be found sitting in his old place outside the hotel.

43    It was some time before he could understand the strange events that had taken place during his sleep: There had been a revolutionary war; the country was no longer a prisoner of old England; and, instead of being a subject of King George the Third of England, he was now a free citizen of the United States of America. Rip, in fact, was no politician. The changes of states and government leaders made little impression on him. To be sure, he understood and was grateful for his freedom—from Dame Van Winkle. Whenever her name was mentioned, however, he only lifted his shoulders, shook his head, and rolled his eyes.

44    He used to tell his story to every stranger that arrived at the hotel. Some always doubted the reality of it, and insisted that Rip had been out of his head. But nearly all of the old Dutch villagers believed it fully. Even to this day, when they hear a thunderstorm on a summer afternoon in the Catskills, they say that Hendrick Hudson and his crew are at their game of nine-pins. And it is a common wish of all henpecked husbands in the neighborhood, when life hangs heavy on their hands, that they might have a quieting drink out of Rip Van Winkle's cup.

## AFTER YOU READ THE STORY

### A. Understanding the Plot

Answer the following questions with complete sentences.

1. Where and when did Rip Van Winkle live?
2. What was Rip's relationship with his wife like? Why did he go off into the mountains?
3. Why did Rip help the "strange figure" who called his name on the mountain?
4. What was odd about the men who were playing at nine-pins?
5. Where and why did Rip fall asleep?
6. Name three things that Rip found surprising or puzzling just after he awoke. Name three things that he found surprising or puzzling when he returned to the village.
7. What had happened in the world while Rip slept?
8. What did Peter Vanderdonk tell the crowd about Hendrick Hudson?
9. How did Rip spend his last years?

### B. Understanding Words in Context

"Rip Van Winkle" contains many idioms that you can understand only by guessing their meaning from the context in which they appear. In this exercise, you are asked to complete the following sentences by choosing the idiom (**a, b,** or **c**) that makes the best sense in the context of the sentence. The sentences are not from the story, but all the idioms are. A paragraph number follows each idiom so that you can check your understanding of its meaning in the context of the story.

1. Jack seems unable to keep a job. Last year, he worked for three different companies, but for only three months total. He wears old clothes and has no car. It doesn't seem to bother him, though. Apparently, he'd rather
   **a.** eat white bread than brown. (6)
   **b.** lift his shoulders than roll his eyes. (6)
   **c.** go hungry on a penny than work for a dollar. (6)

2. Suzie isn't a friend of mine any more. We both left our car doors unlocked, but when her stereo was stolen,
   a. Suzie laid the blame on me. (4)
   b. Suzie hung on my coat. (4)
   c. Suzie took my side. (4)

3. The Committee for the Revolution tried to plan a secret meeting, but their meeting was ruined when government soldiers
   a. kept it in order. (5)
   b. broke in on it. (8)
   c. played tricks on it. (4)

4. I walk to the seashore and sit quietly looking out at the waves when I am unhappy or feel that
   a. life hangs heavy on my hands. (44)
   b. a tongue is the edged tool that grows sharper with frequent use. (7)
   c. my eyes are swimming in my head. (15)

5. When she reached the top of the mountain, completely out of breath (9), she enjoyed the view, although
   a. her tongue was going non-stop. (6)
   b. this was a dog's life (8) and she was an empty shell. (22)
   c. she was definitely the worse for wear because of the steep climb. (42)

## C. Close Reading: Henpecked Husband and Shrewish Wife

The henpecked husband and the shrewish wife are character types that appear in the folk stories of many different countries and cultures. Much of the humor in "Rip Van Winkle" comes from the clever, often indirect or ironic way in which Irving presents Rip and Dame Van Winkle. Show your understanding of Irving's ironic humor by answering the following questions with direct quotations from the story. Paragraph numbers are given to guide your rereading.

1. What might Rip's "mildness of spirit" have come from? (3)
2. How do we know that Rip's dislike of "profitable work" does *not* come from a lack of patience? How do we know it does not come from a lack of energy? (5)

3. Which side of the house belonged to Rip, and why? (6)
4. As time passed, what became of Dame Van Winkle's bitter heart and sharp tongue? (7)
5. Why did Dame Van Winkle direct her anger at the members of the philosophers' club that met under the tree in front of the inn? (8)
6. After he returned to the village, Rip was saddened by the changes in his home and friends, and puzzled by almost everything. One bit of news, however, brought him "some comfort." What was it? (32–39)
7. What did other henpecked husbands think of Rip's long sleep in the mountains? (44)

## D. Vocabulary Practice

A **compound word** is formed by joining two words together, often with a hyphen (-); its meaning is a combination of the meaning of the two words that form it. Below are three groups of such words from "Rip Van Winkle." With a partner or in a small group, discuss the meaning of these words in the story (paragraph numbers are given to show where in the story the word first appears). Then, working alone, choose *one* group of words (A, B, or C) and include each of the six words of the group in sentences of your own. Try to write sentences that demonstrate the meaning of the compound word included.

**Example:** good-hearted
He was a good-hearted man who was kind to old people and took care of animals in need of help.

| A | B | C |
|---|---|---|
| time-worn (3) | weather-beaten (3) | good-natured (3) |
| war-like (3) | henpecked (3) | sharp-tongued (3) |
| falling-down (5) | easygoing (6) | innkeeper (7) |
| fellow-sufferer (8) | overlook (9) | square-built (11) |
| thunder-shower (11) | odd-looking (12) | high-heeled (12) |
| overpowered (15) | self-important (25) | by-standers (33) |

1. _____
2. _____
3. _____

**4.** _____

**5.** _____

**6.** _____

## E. Word Forms

Study the word-form chart below. Notice that for each verb there are two noun forms; one expresses the idea or concept of the verb, the other is used for the person who performs the action of the verb. In the sentences that follow, fill in the blanks with the correct forms of each word given.

| Noun | Verb | Adjective | Adverb |
|------|------|-----------|--------|
| colony, colonist | colonize | colonial | |
| complaint, complainer | complain | complaining | complainingly |
| descent, descendant | descend | descending, descended | |
| frequency, frequenter | frequent | frequent | frequently |
| philosophy, philosopher | philosophize | philosophical | philosophically |

1. *(colonize)* The Dutch were the first _____ in the Hudson River valley; but by the time our story begins, this part of the country was a _____ of England.

2. *(complain)* Dame Winkle was a great _____, but when she _____ the loudest, Rip simply rolled his eyes and walked outside.

3. *(descend)* Peter Vanderdonk was _____ from a famous historian; so the village people believed him when he said that the strange mountain men were Hendrick Hudson's crew, or perhaps their _____.

4. *(frequent)* Rip was a _____ visitor to a particular spot in front of the old inn; and even after his return from the mountains, he could _____ be seen sitting there and telling visitors his story.

5. *(philosophize)* They said that Nicholas Vedder was born with a pipe in his mouth and _____ in his blood; but Rip was born only with a _____ attitude toward work.

## F. Discussion: A Good Time to Be Asleep?

1. Do you ever want to be asleep instead of doing what you are doing? What kind of activity makes you feel this way? Do you know someone who has said he or she wished to sleep instead of facing an unpleasant situation or a difficult person? Explain.

2. Have you ever actually slept through an important event? What was it? How did you feel when you woke up? Can you think of an event in your life that you wish you had slept through, but didn't? What was it?

3. In Irving's story, Rip Van Winkle sleeps through twenty years of American history that brought far-reaching and sometimes violent change to the country. From what you know about Rip from the story, what events or changes do you think he was happy to miss? What events or changes may he have regretted missing?

## G. Language Activity: Legends

A legend is a story about a wonderful or unusual event; the story is handed down from one generation to another over the years. A legend often has a historical basis, but one that cannot be proved. Often, the story becomes more and more amazing as it is passed down through the years. In "Rip Van Winkle," Irving uses a legend about the old Dutch settlers in the Hudson River valley. Characters from this legend appear to Rip (paragraphs 10–15 in the story), and the "historical basis" of the legend is later presented by old Mr. Vanderdonk (paragraph 41).

Can you think of a legend about the place where you were born or grew up? Can you think of a legend about the place where you now live, if it is not the same place where you were born or grew up? Do you know any legends about other places? Work with a small group of classmates to compare the legends you know, and choose one to tell to the whole class. If you cannot think of a legend that you have heard of yourself, try to remember a story about the distant past that you may have read about in school or heard from a parent or grandparent.

## H. Writing: Description

Complete one of the following two writing exercises. Before doing the exercise, review the lists of compound words in Exercise D. Try to use at least two or three of those words in your description.

1. Choose a person who (like Rip Van Winkle) is well-known in your home town or city, or in your current neighborhood or apartment building. Describe what the person looks like (face, body, clothes), and also tell why he or she is so well known. Say whether the person is liked or disliked, admired or feared, respected or joked about by other people. End your description by giving your own personal opinion about the person you have chosen.

2. In "Rip Van Winkle," Irving describes parts of the village, and the countryside near it, both before and after Rip's twenty-year sleep. (For example, see paragraphs 2, 7, 9, and 11 for "before," and paragraphs 18, 19, 22, and 23 for "after.")

Choose a place you know well—countryside, village, town, or city—and write a description of how it looked both before and after a period of change (the period does not have to be twenty years). Write no fewer than 150 and no more than 300 words. Consider the following questions before you begin writing.

a. Before the period of change, if you stood in one particular spot in the place you have chosen and turned in a complete circle, what would you have seen?

b. What feelings did you experience when you looked at this place?

c. What brought change to the place you have chosen?

d. After the period of change, if you stood in the same spot and turned in a complete circle, what would you see? Give details of the changes you see. How did those changes in the look of the place make you feel?

## 5

# THE WIVES OF THE DEAD

✳

### Adapted from the story by
### NATHANIEL HAWTHORNE

Nathaniel Hawthorne was born in Salem, Massachusetts, in 1804. His ancestors were among the earliest settlers in New England. Hawthorne became interested in the history and moral beliefs of these earliest settlers as a young man. He began to write stories in the years right after graduating from college in 1825, but publication followed slowly. Two important collections were published: *Twice-Told Tales* (1835, enlarged in 1842) and *Mosses from an Old Manse*[1] (1846). Although his talents were recognized by literary figures of this period, like Edgar Allan Poe and Henry Wadsworth Longfellow, Hawthorne's books sold very little, and he took jobs in the Custom House in Boston and later in Salem. In 1850, he published *The Scarlet Letter*, which brought him fame. The 1850s were very creative years for Hawthorne. As well as novels and stories, he published a biography of the new U.S. president, Franklin Pierce, who had been a college friend. Pierce recognized Hawthorne's work by appointing him U.S. consul to Liverpool, England, where he served from 1853 to 1857. He then traveled in France and Italy. He returned to Concord, Massachusetts, in 1860, where he lived until his

---

[1] moss = low greenish plant seen on old stone; manse = a large old house; the word was
originally used for the home of a minister

death in 1864. Hawthorne writes about opposing ideas, or themes, that affect human life: the past opposed to the present, moral duty opposed to emotions, reality opposed to imagination. His stories often present a problem, or mystery, that readers must solve for themselves. But Hawthorne writes about his characters with great sympathy. They are believable people, not lifeless symbols of complex themes.

## BEFORE YOU READ THE STORY

### A. About the Author

Read the paragraph about Nathaniel Hawthorne on page 69. Why did Hawthorne take jobs in Boston and Salem? Which book made Hawthorne famous? The paragraph notes three "opposing ideas, or themes" that appear in many of his stories. What are they?

### B. The Pictures

Look at the picture on page 72. Describe the expressions on the faces of the two women. Do they look happy? Sad? Tired? Angry? How are they dressed? Where are they sitting? The picture on page 77 shows the same two women. How are they dressed now?

### C. Thinking About a Person's Death

Consider the title of the story: "The Wives of the Dead." What can we assume will be one theme of the story? Think about the strong emotion we feel when someone close to us dies. How do we try to find, or give, comfort in this case? There are ways we may try to keep the memory of a loved person with us after death. What are some of these ways?

### D. Scanning for Important Dates

Sometimes we can organize information about a person's life by taking note of the dates when important events occurred. Scan the paragraph on Hawthorne's life on page 69 and note what happened during the following years:

1. 1804 _____

2. 1825 _____

3. 1835 _____

4. 1850 _____

5. 1853–1857 _____

6. 1860 _____

7. 1864 _____

# THE WIVES OF THE DEAD

The following story of a simple, domestic incident may not seem worth relating after so many years. A hundred years ago, however, it awakened some interest in the largest seaport town of Massachusetts.

2     It was the rainy evening of an autumn day in a parlor on the second floor of a small house. The house was plainly furnished, as suited its inhabitants, yet decorated with little curiosities from beyond the sea. These, then, were the scene and the season. Two young, lovely women sat together by the fireplace nursing their shared sorrow. They were the recent brides of two brothers, a sailor and a landsman. On the two previous days, word had been brought of their

husbands' deaths. One had been killed in the war in Canada, the other in a storm at sea.

3    Sympathy for their bereavement brought many consoling guests to the parlor of the widows. Several, the minister among them, remained until evening. Then, one by one, whispering comfortable blessings from the Bible, the visitors departed for their own happier homes. The widows, though they recognized their friends' kindness, longed to be alone. They had been united by the relationship of their living husbands; they felt even closer through their relationship to the dead. Each felt that whatever consolation was possible could come only from the other. They joined their hearts, and grieved together silently.

4    One of the sisters-in-law, Mary, was a mild, quiet, though not weak, character. After an hour, she began to recall the lessons of resignation and endurance her religion had taught her before she had need for them. Besides, she thought, since she had heard earliest of her misfortune, she should earliest return to her regular duties. She placed the table before the fireplace and arranged a simple meal. Then she took the hand of her companion.

5    "Come, dearest Margaret. You have eaten nothing today. Come, let us ask a blessing on the food provided for us."

6    Her sister-in-law was of a lively and expressive character. The first pain of her sorrow had been expressed with cries and passionate groans. Now she turned away from Mary's consoling words.

7    "There is no blessing left for me, nor will I ask it," cried Margaret. "I wish it were God's will that I might never eat again."

8    Yet she trembled at her rebellious words, and, by degrees, Mary was able to bring Margaret's emotions nearer to her own. Time went on, and the usual hour of sleep arrived.

9    The brothers and their brides had married on small earnings, and therefore had joined households. They shared the parlor, and had two bedrooms that led into it. Into these the widows retired, first placing a lighted lamp by the fireplace. The doors of both rooms were left open, so that the beds, with their unclosed curtains, were in sight of both women.

10    Sleep did not come to the sisters-in-law at the same
time. Mary experienced the result of quiet grief and soon
sank back into temporary forgetfulness. But Margaret
became more disturbed as the night advanced into its
deepest and stillest hours. She lay listening to the drops of
rain that fell continuously, and kept lifting her head to look
into Mary's bedroom and the parlor. The cold light of the
lamp threw the shadows of the furniture up against the wall.
Two empty armchairs were in their old positions on
opposite sides of the fireplace where the brothers used to sit,
as heads of families. Two smaller chairs were near them—
the true thrones of that little domestic kingdom. Here Mary
and Margaret had ruled with love, with the power that love
had given. The cheerful light of the fire had shone on their
happy circle. The dead glow of the lamp might have lighted
their reunion now. While Margaret groaned in bitterness,
she heard a knock at the street door.

11    "How my heart would have leapt yesterday," she
thought. "I care not for it now; let them go away—I will
not get up."

12    But even as she spoke, she was breathing hurriedly and
listening to hear if the knocking was repeated. It is difficult
to believe in the death of someone as close to us as
ourselves. The knocking continued, slow and regular; a
voice was faintly heard through the wall. Margaret looked
into Mary's room and saw her still lying in the depths of
sleep. Margaret arose, trembling with fear and eagerness.

13    "Heaven help me!" she sighed. "I have nothing left to
fear, and yet I am more a coward than ever."

14    She took up the lamp from the fireplace and hurried to
the window which overlooked the street door. She stretched
her head a little way into the rainy air. Outside, another
lamp cast reddish light on the front of the house, while
darkness buried every other object. As the window opened,
a man in a broad hat and heavy coat stepped into the light
and looked up. Margaret recognized him as the friendly
innkeeper of the town.

15    "What is it, Goodman Parker?" asked the widow.

16    "Ah, well—is it you, Mistress Margaret?" replied the
innkeeper. "I was afraid it might be your sister-in-law,
Mary. I hate to see a young woman in trouble, when I
haven't a word of consolation to whisper her."

17    "For Heaven's sake, what news do you bring?" Margaret cried out.

18    "Why, a messenger with letters from the Governor came through town just now from the Canadian border. He stopped at my inn for food and drink, and I asked him news of the Canadian wars. He tells me we won the battle you know of, and that thirteen men reported killed are alive and well—your husband among them. I thought you wouldn't mind being awakened, so I stepped over to tell you."

19    So saying, the good man departed. His lamp glowed along the street, lighting the dark shapes of things, like order shining through chaos, or memory looking over the past. But Margaret did not stay to watch. Joy leapt into her heart and lightened it at once. Breathless, she flew to tell Mary the news. She paused at Mary's door, however, while a thought of pain broke in upon her.

20    "Poor Mary!" she said to herself. "Shall I wake her, to feel her grief sharpened by my happiness? No. I will keep the news until tomorrow."

21    Margaret approached the bed to discover if Mary's sleep were peaceful. A look of motionless calm lay on Mary's face, as if her heart was a deep lake, now grown calm because its dead had sunk so far down into it. It is fortunate, though strange, that dreams are created mostly from the lighter sorrows. Margaret couldn't disturb her sister-in-law. With a sudden step she turned away. But her joy could not be quieted. Her mind was full of delightful thoughts till sleep transformed them into dreams. These bloomed delightful and wild, like winter frost (but what a cold comparison!) making flowers and leaves on the window-glass.

22    When night was far advanced, Mary woke up suddenly. A dream had caught her in its unreal life, and for a time sleep hung round her like a morning mist. She could not tell where she was. Slowly she became aware of rapid, eager knocking at the door. Slowly she became aware that the knocking was an order to be obeyed. At the same moment, the pain of remembering leapt to her mind and the mist of sleep fell from her grieving face. Fearing that Margaret would be disturbed, she hurried into the parlor, took the lamp from the fireplace and went to the window. By some accident, it had been left unlocked, and opened easily.

23     "Who's there?" asked Mary, trembling as she looked out.

24     The storm was over, and the moon was up. It shone on broken clouds above, and on black houses below. A young man stood under the window. He was dressed in sailors' clothes, as wet as if he had come from the depths of the sea. Mary recognized him—he worked on a ship that made short voyages along the coast. Before her marriage, he had unsuccessfully asked to marry her himself.

25     "What do you seek here, Stephen?" she said.

26     "Cheer up, Mary, for I seek to comfort you," answered the rejected lover. "I got home just ten minutes ago, and the first thing my good mother told me was the news about your husband. So, without saying a word, I threw on my hat and ran out of the house. I couldn't have slept at all before speaking to you, Mary."

27     "Stephen, I thought better of you!" cried Mary, rejecting thought of his renewed interest in her. She began to close the window.

28     "Stop! Hear my story!" cried the young sailor. "I tell you, we spoke to a ship yesterday, coming here from Old England. And who do you think I saw standing on deck, safe and well?"

29     Mary leaned out of the window, but could not speak.

30     "Why, it was your husband himself," continued the generous sailor. "When his own ship sank in the storm, he and three others saved themselves. They caught onto a piece of wood, and floated until they were rescued. The rescue ship will be here by daylight. You'll see him tomorrow. There's the comfort I bring you, Mary, and so good night."

31     He hurried away. Mary watched him in doubt of her waking reality. Her doubt grew stronger or weaker as he passed into the shade of houses or appeared into moonlight. Gradually, however, a blessed confidence filled her heart.

32     Her first thought was to awaken her sister-in-law, and relate her new-born gladness. She opened the bedroom door, which had been closed during the night. She came to Margaret's bedside, and was about to lay her hand on the sleeper's shoulder. But then she remembered that Margaret would awake to thoughts of death and grief, made more bitter when compared with Mary's own happiness. She let

the lamp light fall on the sleeping form of the bereaved one. The bedclothes were twisted all around her. Her young cheeks were rosy and her lips half open in a smile. An expression of joy struggled forth from her face.

33　　"My poor sister! You will wake too soon from that happy dream," thought Mary.

34　　Before retiring, she set down the lamp, and tried to arrange the bedclothes so that the damp air might not harm the sleeper. But her hand trembled against Margaret's neck, a tear also fell upon her cheek, and she suddenly awoke.

## AFTER YOU READ THE STORY

### A. Understanding the Plot

Answer the following questions with complete sentences.

1. Where and when did the events of the story take place?
2. How are the two women related? What did their husbands do for a living?
3. How did their husbands die?
4. When Margaret goes to the window, whom does she find there? What does he tell her?
5. When Mary goes to the window, whom does she find there? What does he tell her?
6. Why does neither woman wake the other to tell her what news the men have brought?

### B. Understanding Words in Context

In the following quotations from the story, one word is underlined. After considering the word in its context, and without looking it up in a dictionary, choose the word or phrase that gives the best sense of the underlined word. Be prepared to explain why you chose it.

1. *Her sister-in-law was of a lively and <u>expressive</u> character. The first pain of her sorrow had been expressed with cries and passionate groans.* (6)
   a. easily showing her feelings
   b. talkative and happy
   c. sad and unhappy

2. *"There is no blessing left for me, nor will I ask it," cried Margaret. "I wish it were God's will that I might never eat again." . . . Yet she trembled at her <u>rebellious</u> words . . .* (7–8)
   a. religious
   b. refusing to be controlled
   c. shaking with fear

3. *The cheerful light of the fire had shone on their happy circle. The dead glow of the lamp might have lighted their <u>reunion</u>.* (10)
   a. storytelling
   b. dancing
   c. being together again

4. *Outside, another lamp <u>cast</u> reddish light on the front of the house, while darkness buried every other object.* (14)
   a. threw
   b. reflected
   c. forced

5. *His lamp glowed along the street, lighting the dark shapes of things, like order shining through <u>chaos</u>, or memory looking over the past.* (19)
   a. peacefulness
   b. confusion
   c. logic

6. *[Margaret's dreams] bloomed delightful and wild, like winter <u>frost</u> (but what a cold comparison!) making flowers and leaves on the window-glass.* (21)
   a. icy patterns
   b. storms
   c. frozen plants

## C. Close Reading: Different Characters, Different Emotions

Hawthorne shows us the opposing personalities of the two women by describing their emotional reactions to the events of the story. Use words or phrases from the story to answer the following questions and show your understanding of these differences. Paragraph numbers are given to guide your rereading.

MARY

**Example:** How does Hawthorne describe Mary? (4)

<u>She was "a mild, quiet, though not weak, character."</u>

1. What lessons has Mary learned from her religion? (4) _____
   _____

2. Why does Mary feel she should return to her ordinary duties earlier than Margaret? (4) _____
   _____

3. What does Mary encourage Margaret to do?  (4–5) _____

_____

4. How does Mary react to falling asleep that night?  (10) ___

_____

5. What mood is Mary in when she wakes up that night?  (22)

_____

6. When she sees Stephen below the window, why does Mary cry, "Stephen, I thought better of you!"?  (26–27) _____

_____

MARGARET

1. How does Hawthorne describe Margaret?  (6) _____

_____

2. How does Margaret react to news of her husband's death? (6) _____

_____

3. What does Margaret mean when she says, "I wish it were God's will that I might never eat again."?  How does she react to her own words?  (7–8) _____

_____

4. What mood is Margaret in as she tries to fall asleep?  (10)

_____

5. What does Margaret say when she hears a visitor knocking at her window?  What does she mean?  (12–13) _____

_____

_____

## D. Vocabulary Practice

Many words have more than one meaning, and the particular meaning of such words must be understood from their context in a sentence. The word *suit* as in "I bought a new <u>suit</u> to wear to my job interview," is a noun meaning a jacket with matching dress pants or skirt. However, in this sentence from the story, *"The house was plainly furnished, as <u>suited</u> its inhabitants"* (2), *suit* is a verb meaning to "fit, please, or satisfy."

In the sentences below, sentence **a** shows one common meaning of the underlined word. Sentence **b**, taken from the story, shows another, less common meaning of the word. Try to guess the meaning of each. Then use a dictionary to check your answers.

1. *(relate)*

   **a.** I have trouble <u>relating</u> to my new boss—I felt more comfortable with my old boss.

   *Relating* means _____

   **b.** *The following story . . . may not seem worth <u>relating</u> after so many years.* (1)

   *Relating* means _____

2. *(nursing)*

   **a.** My cousin goes to <u>nursing</u> school in Boston, Massachusetts, and plans to work for a hospital there.

   *Nursing* means _____

   **b.** *Two young, lovely women sat together by the fireplace, <u>nursing</u> their shared sorrow.* (2)

   *Nursing* means _____

3. *(curiosity)*

   **a.** I hope I never lose my <u>curiosity</u> about new people and new places.

*Curiosity* means _____

**b.** *The house was . . . decorated with little <u>curiosities</u> from beyond the sea.* (2)

*Curiosities* means _____

**4.** *(long)*

    **a.** My grandparents live a <u>long</u> distance from my house.

    *Long* means _____

    **b.** *The widows, though they recognized their friends' kindness, <u>longed</u> to be alone.* (3)

    *Longed* means _____

**5.** *(resignation)*

    **a.** I will give my old boss a letter of <u>resignation</u> before I move on to my new job.

    *Resignation* means _____

    **b.** *After an hour, she began to recall the lessons of <u>resignation</u> and endurance her religion taught her . . .* (4)

    *Resignation* means _____

**6.** *(retire)*

    **a.** My parents <u>retired</u> from their jobs when they turned sixty-five.

    *Retired* means _____

    **b.** *Into these [bedrooms] the widows <u>retired</u>, first placing a lighted lamp by the fireplace.* (9)

    *Retired* means _____

## E. Word Forms

| Noun | Verb | Adjective |
|------|------|-----------|
| consolation | console | consoling |
| endurance | endure | enduring |
| grief | grieve | grieving |
| inhabitant | inhabit | inhabited |
| rebellion | rebel | rebellious |
| rejection | reject | rejected |

For each group of three sentences below, choose a word (with its three different forms) from the chart and place the correct forms of the word in the blank spaces provided. Each word on the chart fits only one group of three sentences. When entering the verb form, make sure you use the correct tense. The first one has been done for you.

1.  a. Margaret's **rejection** of God's blessing for the food Mary prepared was caused by deep grief.

    b. Although he was a **rejected** lover, Stephen generously brought good news to Mary.

    c. The sisters-in-law did not **reject** the consolation of their friends, but they needed to grieve alone.

2.  a. Margaret _____ more expressively.

    b. Mary's _____ was equally deep.

    c. Margaret could not fall asleep. The _____ widow thought of her husband and groaned in bitterness.

3.  a. On this dark and rainy night, the unlit houses of the town did not look _____.

    b. The innkeeper and Stephen are both _____ of the town.

    c. Mary and Margaret _____ their house since their marriages.

4. a. The two husbands _____ many hardships in their work as soldier and sailor.

 b. Mary felt she had learned the lesson of _____ from her religion.

 c. Thoughts of their husbands' deaths brought the two women _____ grief.

5. a. The minister was among the friends who tried to _____ the widows.

 b. Margaret was too unhappy to find _____ in her religion.

 c. Mary's _____ words helped Margaret to become calmer.

6. a. Perhaps Mary understands Margaret's _____ words better than the minister could.

 b. Stephen probably _____ at Mary's decision that she would marry someone else, but he had to accept her answer.

 c. _____ is in some ways the opposite of resignation.

## F. Discussion: Reality or Dream?

Some readers and critics believe "The Wives of the Dead" is an example of realism. Two women who believe their husbands are dead receive the joyous news that the men are still alive. Other readers and critics believe that the story describes a dream. That is, the two women want so desperately to believe that their husbands are alive that they dream the visits of the innkeeper and Stephen and the good news they bring. What do you think of this possibility? Read over the following questions about the story, then in pairs or small groups choose two of them to study closely. Report your opinions and conclusions to the class.

1. Read the description of the innkeeper's visit again (paragraphs 14–19). Notice how he moves in and out of the light. In what way is this description realistic? In what way does it seem like a dream?

2. Read the last sentence in paragraph 21 again. Hawthorne compares Margaret's dreams to frost flowers on the window glass. Do you think this is a strange image to use, after he has just told us that ". . . *her joy could not be quieted. Her mind was full of delightful thoughts . . .*"? Why, or why not? Why might Hawthorne have chosen this "cold comparison" (as he himself calls it) of happy dreams to frost flowers?

3. Read paragraphs 21 and 22 again. How is Mary sleeping? What does Hawthorne mean when he says that ". . . *dreams are created mostly from the lighter sorrows*"? Do you agree with this? Why or why not? How does Mary wake up? Is she really awake?

4. Read the final paragraph again. Why does Mary's hand "*tremble against Margaret's neck*"? We read ". . . *a tear also fell upon her cheek, and she suddenly awoke.*" Is it clear whose cheek the tear fell upon? What do you think? Is it clear who awoke and why?

## G. Language Activity: Light and Dark

Hawthorne uses light and dark throughout the story to give us a sense of the characters' moods. Read the story again, underlining phrases in which light (fire, lamp, moon) and dark (night, shadow) appear. Working with a partner, compare the phrases each of you underlined, and discuss the meaning of light and dark as you answer the following questions.

1. In paragraph 10 we read, "*The cold light of the lamp threw the shadows of the furniture up against the wall.*" Later, we read, "*The dead glow of the lamp might have lighted their reunion now.*" How does the lamplight relate to Margaret's mood?

2. In paragraph 14 we read, *"Outside, another lamp cast reddish light on the front of the house, while darkness buried every other object. As the window opened, a man in a broad hat and heavy coat stepped into the light and looked up."* What sensations are associated with the color red? Why does the reddish light shine on the house? What color light does the man step into? How does this description show that Margaret's mood is changing?

3. In paragraph 24 we read, *"The storm was over, and the moon was up. It shone on broken clouds above, and on black houses below."* Hawthorne is describing a change in the weather. What has the weather been like? How is it changing? How does this description relate to Mary's mood?

4. In paragraph 31 we read, *"Mary watched him in doubt of her waking reality. Her doubt grew stronger or weaker as he passed into the shade of houses or appeared into moonlight."* Hawthorne's phrases about dark and light reflect changes in Mary's mood after hearing Stephen's news. What are these changes?

## H. Writing: Real or Imagined—The Effects of Strong Emotion

Choose one of the following topics and write three paragraphs, for a total of 150 to 250 words.

1. Have you ever felt an emotion so strong—loss, anger, disappointment, joy, surprise—that you acted in a manner completely unlike yourself? Write about your experience and what you learned about yourself from it. In paragraph 1, describe what caused your strong emotion, and how you reacted, and why. In paragraph 2, tell how you expressed this strong emotion in action and what effect your actions had on others. In paragraph 3, write about how you felt afterward.

2. Have you ever felt so strongly about something, or been so sure about something, that you knew you were right—but later discovered you were wrong? Write about this strong

emotion or conviction, and how you came to see your error. In paragraph 1, describe what you were so sure of and why. In paragraph 2, tell how you discovered your mistake. In paragraph 3, tell how you felt afterward. Did you do something to set things right? What did you do?

3. Continue Hawthorne's story beyond its ending, to make a new one. Write what happens after ". . . *she suddenly awoke.*" In paragraph 35, make it clear who "she" is, and what both women are doing when "she" awakes. In paragraph 36, describe what has actually happened during the night. In paragraph 37, conclude your story by writing about what will happen next.

*6*

# NINE NEEDLES

✳

### A story by
### JAMES THURBER

James Thurber was born in Columbus, Ohio, in 1894. He went to school and university there. The loss of sight in one eye as a boy kept him from active military duty in World War I, but he did serve in Europe as a State Department clerk. After some years as a reporter in Ohio and New York, he went to live in Paris (as did many American writers and artists of his generation, especially in the 1920s) and remained there for two years, 1924–1926. He then returned to New York and began his career as a humorist for a new magazine called *The New Yorker*. *The New Yorker* published a mixture of cartoons, essays, humorous and serious short stories, and articles—often ironic—on events and lifestyles in America's largest city. *The New Yorker* became, and still is, the most famous weekly magazine of its kind in the United States. Thurber had started drawing pictures even before he began to write, and *The New Yorker* published his drawings, cartoons, essays, humorous fables, and short stories for the next thirty-five years. Thurber also wrote plays and children's stories. Thurber's eyesight began failing in the 1940s, and by the time of his death in 1961, he was almost completely blind. Thurber's humor explores the strangeness and even "craziness" hidden behind everyday activities and events that we usually think of as simple or ordinary. Like most great humorists, he can make us laugh at matters that in real life might be serious, sad, awkward, or terrifying.

## BEFORE YOU READ THE STORY

### A. About the Author

Read the paragraph about James Thurber on page 89. What different forms did his work take, and why was *The New Yorker* such a good fit for them? What is Thurber's view of everyday activities that we think of as ordinary?

### B. The Picture

The picture on page 92 was drawn by Thurber and is typical of his line drawings. What is the man holding over his head? (Note the **caption**, or words under the picture.) What do you think he is about to do with it?

### C. Thinking About What's Funny and Why

Do you think the picture on page 92 is funny? Can you say why or why not? Do you think that everyone in your family would agree that it was or wasn't funny? Do you and all your friends usually agree on what's funny? When two people do not agree on what's funny, do you think the difference is usually a difference of age, culture, or personality? What makes you think so?

### D. Scanning Different Sources of Information

For this exercise, you will need to use the paragraphs about James Thurber (page 89), Edith Wharton (page 29), Washington Irving (page 47), and Nathaniel Hawthorne (page 69). To find answers to the questions below, let your eyes move rapidly over the four paragraphs looking for the particular information you want. Make notes as you go. Try to complete the exercise in less than five minutes.

1. Which of the writers was born first?
2. Which of the writers died last?
3. Which of the writers died youngest?
4. Which of the writers died oldest?
5. Which writer lived mostly outside of the United States?
6. Which of the writers held at least one job that was not involved with literature or writing?

A **medicine cabinet**, or **chest**, like the one pictured on page 92, is usually not found above the head of an angry man, but rather on a wall over the sink or **washbowl** in a bathroom. In some homes, these cabinets are sometimes crowded, or **cluttered** with many objects beside medicine. In Thurber's story, a man cuts himself shaving while visiting friends and needs a **styptic pencil**, a medical item shaped like a pencil and used to stop bleeding from small cuts. He opens the medicine cabinet to look for one—and the adventure begins.

# NINE NEEDLES

One of the more spectacular minor happenings of the past few years which I am sorry that I missed took place in Columbus, Ohio, home of some friends of a friend of mine. It seems that a Mr. Albatross, while looking for something in his medicine cabinet one morning, discovered a bottle of a kind of patent medicine[1] which his wife had been taking for a stomach ailment. Now, Mr. Albatross is one of those apprehensive men who are afraid of patent medicines and of almost everything else. Some weeks before, he had encountered a paragraph in a Consumers' Research bulletin which announced that this particular medicine was bad for you. He had thereupon ordered his wife to throw out what was left of her supply of the stuff and never buy any more. She had promised, and here now was another bottle of the perilous liquid. Mr. Albatross, a man given to quick rages, shouted the conclusion of the story at my friend: "I threw the bottle out the bathroom window and the medicine chest after it!" It seems to me that must have been a spectacle worth going a long way to see.

2    I am sure that many a husband has wanted to wrench the family medicine cabinet off the wall and throw it out the

---

[1] patent medicine = a medicine made of "secret" ingredients and often sold outside of regular pharmacies or drugstores

*"And the Medicine Chest After It!"*

window, if only because the average medicine cabinet is so filled with mysterious bottles and unidentifiable objects of all kinds that it is a source of constant bewilderment and exasperation to the American male. Surely the British medicine cabinet and the French medicine cabinet and all the other medicine cabinets must be simpler and better ordered than ours. It may be that the American habit of saving everything and never throwing anything away, not even empty bottles, causes the domestic medicine cabinet to become as cluttered in its small way as the American attic becomes cluttered in its major way. I have encountered few medicine cabinets in this country which were not pack-jammed[2] with something between a hundred and fifty and two hundred different items, from dental floss to boracic acid, from razor blades to sodium perborate, from adhesive tape to coconut oil.[3] Even the neatest wife will put off cleaning out the medicine cabinet on the ground that[4] she has something else to do that is more important at the moment, or more diverting. It was in the apartment of such a wife and her husband that I became enormously involved with a medicine cabinet not long ago.

3    I had spent the weekend with this couple—they live on East Tenth Street near Fifth Avenue—such a weekend as left me reluctant to rise up on Monday morning with bright and shining face and go to work. They got up and went to work, but I didn't. I didn't get up until about two thirty in the afternoon. I had my face all lathered for shaving and the washbowl was full of hot water when suddenly I cut myself with the razor. I cut my ear. Very few men cut themselves with razors, but I do, possibly because I was taught the old Spencerian free-wrist movement[5] by my writing teacher in the grammar grades. The ear bleeds rather profusely when cut with a razor and is difficult to get at. More angry than hurt, I jerked open the door of the medicine cabinet to see if I could find a styptic pencil and out fell, from the top shelf, a little black paper packet containing nine needles. It seems that this wife kept a little paper packet containing nine needles on the top shelf of the

---

[2] pack-jammed = very full; the modern expression is *jam-packed*
[3] boracic acid, sodium perborate, and coconut oil = medicines used for cleaning, disinfecting, or calming skin problems
[4] on the ground that = because, or using the excuse that
[5] the old Spenserian free-wrist movement = a handwriting technique developed in the 1800s by a man named P.R. Spenser

medicine cabinet. The packet fell into the soapy water of the washbowl, where the paper rapidly disintegrated, leaving nine needles at large[6] in the bowl. I was, naturally enough, not in the best condition, either physical or mental, to recover nine needles from a washbowl. No gentleman who has lather on his face and whose ear is bleeding is in the best condition for anything, even something involving the handling of nine blunt objects.

4     It did not seem wise for me to pull the plug out of the washbowl and let the needles go down the drain. I had visions of clogging up the plumbing system of the house, and also a vague fear of causing short circuits[7] somehow or other (I know very little about electricity and I don't want to have it explained to me). Finally I groped very gently around the bowl and eventually had four of the needles in the palm of one hand and three in the palm of another—two I couldn't find. If I had thought quickly and clearly, I wouldn't have done that. A lathered man whose ear is bleeding and who has four wet needles in one hand and three in the other may be said to have reached the lowest point of human efficiency. There is nothing he can do but stand there. I tried transferring the needles in my left hand to the palm of my right hand, but I couldn't get them off my left hand. Wet needles cling to you. In the end, I wiped the needles off onto a bathtowel which was hanging on a rod above the bathtub. It was the only towel that I could find. I had to dry my hands afterward on the bathmat. Then I tried to find the needles in the towel. Hunting for seven needles in a bathtowel is the most tedious[8] occupation I have ever engaged in. I could find only five of them. With the two that had been left in the bowl, that meant there were four needles in all missing—two in the washbowl and two others lurking in the towel or lying in the bathtub under the towel. Frightful thoughts came to me of what might happen to anyone who used that towel or washed his face in the sink or got into the tub, if I didn't find the missing needles. Well, I didn't find them. I sat down on the edge of the tub to think, and I decided finally that the only thing to do was

---

[6] at large = dangerously free (idiom)
[7] short circuits = electrical problems
[8] tedious = tiresome, boring

wrap up the towel in a newspaper and take it away with me. I also decided to leave a message for my friends explaining as clearly as I could that I was afraid there were two needles in the bathtub and two needles in the washbowl, and that they better be careful.

5    I looked everywhere in the apartment, but I could not find a pencil, pen or a typewriter. I could find pieces of paper, but nothing with which to write on them. I don't know what gave me the idea—a movie I had seen, perhaps, or a story I had read—but I suddenly thought of writing a message with a lipstick. The wife might have an extra lipstick lying around, and, if so, I concluded it would be in the medicine cabinet. I went back to the medicine cabinet and began poking around in it for a lipstick. I saw what I thought looked like the metal tip of one, and I got two fingers around it and began to pull gently—it was under a lot of things. Every object in the medicine cabinet began to slide. Bottles broke in the washbowl and on the floor; red, brown, and white liquids spurted; nail files, scissors, razor blades, and miscellaneous objects sang and clattered and tinkled. I was covered with perfume, peroxide, and cold cream.

6    It took me half an hour to get the debris[9] all together in the middle of the bathroom floor. I made no attempt to put anything back in the medicine cabinet. I knew it would take a steadier hand than mine and a less shattered spirit. Before I went away (only partly shaved) and abandoned the shambles, I left a note saying that I was afraid there were needles in the bathtub and the washbowl and that I had taken their towel and that I would call up and tell them everything—I wrote it in iodine with the end of a toothbrush. I have not yet called up, I am sorry to say. I have neither found the courage nor thought up the words to explain what happened. I suppose my friends believe that I deliberately smashed up their bathroom and stole their towel. I don't know for sure, because they haven't called me up either.

---

[9] debris = pieces, remains, ruins

## AFTER YOU READ THE STORY

### A. Understanding the Plot

Answer the following questions with complete sentences.

1. Why did Mr. Albatross throw a bottle and a medicine cabinet out of his bathroom window?
2. According to Thurber, why are American medicine cabinets so cluttered?
3. What was Thurber looking for when he first opened the medicine cabinet in his friends' house? Why was he looking for this item?
4. Why didn't Thurber pull the plug out of the washbowl and just let the needles go down the drain?
5. Why did Thurber want to write a message to his friends after he got the needles off his hands?
6. What caused bottles to break, liquids to spurt, and other objects to sing and clatter and tinkle?
7. What did Thurber take with him from the bathroom when he left his friends' house, and why? What did he leave behind?

### B. Understanding Words in Context

Choose the word or phrase (**a**, **b**, or **c**) that best defines the underlined word in the following sentences from the story. Look back at the paragraphs to read the word in its full context. After you have made your choice, write down what context clues led you to make it.

**Example:** *Now, Mr. Albatross is one of those <u>apprehensive</u> men who are afraid of patent medicines and of almost everything else.* (1)

    **a.** logical    **b.** fearful    **c.** angry

    <u>We read that he is "afraid . . . of almost everything," so apprehensive must mean fearful.</u>

1. . . . *here now was another bottle of the <u>perilous</u> liquid.*  (1)
   **a.** delicious      **b.** bad-tasting      **c.** dangerous

   _____

   _____

2. . . . *many a husband has wanted to <u>wrench</u> the family medicine cabinet off the wall . . .*  (2)
   **a.** clean out      **b.** pull hard      **c.** hammer

   _____

   _____

3. . . . *it is a source of constant <u>bewilderment and exasperation</u> to the American male.*  (2)
   **a.** wildness and excellence  **b.** seriousness and thoughtfulness
   **c.** confusion and annoyance

   _____

   _____

4. . . . *she has something else to do that is more important at the moment, or more <u>diverting</u>.*  (2)
   **a.** important      **b.** unpleasant      **c.** entertaining

   _____

   _____

5. *The packet fell into the soapy water of the washbowl, where the paper rapidly <u>disintegrated</u>, leaving nine needles at large in the bowl.*  (3)
   **a.** came apart      **b.** sank      **c.** faded

   _____

   _____

**6.** *I had visions of <u>clogging up</u> the plumbing system . . .* (4)

   **a.** stopping up    **b.** starting up    **c.** freeing up

_____

_____

**7.** *. . . there were four needles in all missing—two in the washbowl and two others <u>lurking</u> in the towel or lying in the bathtub under the towel.* (4)

   **a.** cutting    **b.** hiding    **c.** sticking out

_____

_____

**8.** *Before I went away (only partly shaved) and <u>abandoned the shambles</u>, I left a note . . .* (6)

   **a.** cleaned up the objects    **b.** left the mess

   **c.** ruined the bottles

_____

_____

## C. Close Reading: If Only He Hadn't...

In paragraphs 3–5, Thurber shows us how his bathroom disaster happened one small step at a time. If only he hadn't taken one step, the next step wouldn't have occurred. Referring back to those three paragraphs when necessary, choose the *result clause* that best completes each *if clause* below and write its letter in the space provided. The first one has been done for you.

*If* clauses

1. _b_ If only he hadn't gotten out of bed so late that morning,

2. ___ If only he hadn't cut himself while shaving,

3. ___ If only he hadn't opened the medicine chest,

4. ___ If only he hadn't had doubts about the plumbing system and electricity,

5. ___ If only his hands hadn't been so wet and soapy,

6. ___ If only he hadn't decided to write a message with a lipstick,

7. ___ If only he hadn't tried to pull the lipstick from the medicine cabinet,

8. ___ If only he hadn't completely abandoned the shambles in the bathroom

Result clauses

a. he wouldn't have needed to wipe the needles off onto a bathtowel.
b. he wouldn't have been alone without help in his friends' house.
c. he might have found the courage to call up his friends.
d. he wouldn't have looked in the medicine cabinet for a styptic pencil.
e. he wouldn't have gone back to the medicine cabinet and begun poking around in it.
f. everything would not have begun to slide, fall, and break.
g. the packet of needles wouldn't have fallen into the washbowl.
h. he might have pulled the plug and let the needles go down the drain.

## D. Vocabulary Practice

Working with a partner or in a small group, review the meaning of the following one-syllable verbs in the story (paragraph numbers are given to guide you). Then, working alone, choose the verb from the list that best completes the meaning of each sentence, and write it in the blank space, using the correct form.

clog (4)        cling (4)        spurt (5)
grope (4)       lurk (4)         smash (6)
poke (5)        wrench (2)       wrap (4)

1. He tried to slash me with his knife, but I _____ it from his hand and threw it far away.

2. The boy woke from his nightmare and, shaking with fear, _____ around in the dark room until he found the light switch.

3. The magnets _____ to the metal doors.

4. The child was so sure that a ghost was _____ in his closet that he cried out for his parents to come and find it.

5. The young girl _____ the dog with a stick until at last it turned and snapped at her.

6. Because dirt, small stones, and mud _____ all the old water pipes in the village, the water dripped only slowly from the sink faucets.

7. Carrying the ladder on his shoulder and turning to answer a question, Mr. Hardy _____ every glass or china object on the high table behind him.

8. The villager _____ the vegetables and spices in banana leaves and cooked them slowly over low heat.

9. The sunburned old farmer drilled for oil without much hope, but then he watched in amazement as the thick black liquid _____ out of the ground and high into the air above his land.

## E. Word Forms

| Noun | Verb | Adjective/Participle |
|---|---|---|
| bewilderment | bewilder | bewildered, bewildering |
| consumer, consumption | consume | consuming, consumed |
| disintegration | disintegrate | disintegrating, disintegrated |
| diversion | divert | diverting, diverted |
| exasperation | exasperate | exasperating, exasperated |

Two forms of one of the words in the chart above logically complete the meaning of each sentence below.

1. Mr. Albatross thought that the _____ of patent medicines was dangerous, so he wouldn't allow his wife to _____ any of them.

2. "What could be more _____ than to neaten and rearrange all these colored bottles in my medicine cabinet," Mrs. Albatross thought just before the bright sunlight outside her window _____ her attention to the needs of her garden.

3. _____ by the unidentifiable objects and general mess in his medicine cabinet, Mr. Albatross reacted strangely: his _____ turned to anger, and he threw the thing out the bathroom window, almost hitting Mrs. Albatross, cutting flowers below him in the garden.

4. Deep in the soapy water of the washbowl, the _____ paper packet began to release its contents, and when its _____ was complete, nine dangerous needles were at large in the bowl.

5. Thurber's narrator was so _____ by his failure to find all the needles that in the end he left everything for his friends to figure out and clean up; and the reason they did not phone him later may have had something to do with the _____ they felt when they saw what he had done.

## F. Discussion: Clutter

*Clutter* is a pile or collection of things all confused together—a mess of things lying in confusion.

1. Are you the type of person who can live comfortably in a cluttered space, or do you like everything in order, everything neat and well arranged? What about other members of your family or your roommates: Are they alike in this preference, or are they different?

2. Would you describe clutter as a cultural problem? Why, or why not? Can you think of a society or culture where there is either less clutter or more clutter than where you are now living? What causes the difference in the amount of clutter in these two societies or cultures?

## G. Language Activity: What's Funny?

1. Think of a joke in your native language. Try in your head to translate it into English, and then tell it to a small group of classmates. If they don't understand the joke, or simply don't laugh, try to explain why the joke amuses people in your language. Listen to the jokes they tell, and say what you think of them. As a group, tell to the class any jokes that your group thought were at least somewhat funny.
2. Think of a scene from a book, movie, or TV program (in any language) that recently made you smile or laugh. Think carefully about exactly what happened in that scene. Describe the scene to a small group of students. Note how many in the group thought the scene was funny, and report to the whole class.

## H. Writing: A Summary

Write a summary of the actions Thurber describes in paragraphs 3–6. Write in the third person (use "he" and "Thurber," not "I"). In order to write this summary, you must decide which were the most important actions in the scene and which actions and other comments can be left out. It will help you to begin by listing the actions you think are central to the scene. When you write the summary, use conjunctions (*and, but, or*) and adverbial clause connectors (*when, before, after, because*) to show the relationship of one action to another. Try to limit your summary to less than a hundred words. Begin with the following sentence:

> In the story "Nine Needles," a man who is a guest in his friends' house has a strange experience with the medicine cabinet in their bathroom.

# 7

# A MYSTERY OF HEROISM

✳

**Adapted from the story by**

**STEPHEN CRANE**

Stephen Crane was born in 1871 in Newark, New Jersey, the fourteenth and youngest child of a minister. After some schooling at Lafayette College and Syracuse University, he became a journalist in New York City, writing for different newspapers. He lived in great poverty in those early years, and his experiences in the poor sections of New York led to his first novel, *Maggie: A Girl of the Streets,* which he completed when he was only twenty years old. This book was a work of social realism that was very unusual for its time. Crane attempted to present people as they actually were and events as they actually happened, with little or no comment of his own. This realistic (or naturalistic) method was completely new in American literature. In 1895, still only twenty-four, he published *The Red Badge of Courage,* a novel about a frightened young soldier in the American Civil War. This book became a best-seller and is still widely read today. It assured Crane's literary, though not his financial, success. He continued working as a journalist, and his work as a reporter (often about war) took him to Mexico, the American West, Cuba, and Greece. He traveled to England in 1897, settled there briefly, and became friends with well-known writers such as Joseph Conrad, Henry James, and H. G. Wells. But he was suffering from the disease tuberculosis, and in search of a cure he went to Badenweiler, Germany. He died there in 1900. He was only twenty-nine, but his stories, novels, articles, and experimental poetry filled twelve volumes when collected together in 1926.

# BEFORE YOU READ THE STORY

## A. About the Author

Read the paragraph about Stephen Crane on page 105. In what way was Crane's writing new to American literature? What countries outside of the United States did Crane visit or live in, and why did he go to those countries?

## B. The Pictures

Crane's story takes place on a battlefield of the American Civil War (1861–1865). This war between the northern and southern states was fought over the southern states' attempt to separate themselves from the country and form a new one of their own. The war was long and bitter; hundreds of thousands of young men's lives were lost in battles both large and small. The arrangement of the two armies in Crane's story is shown by the map on page 108. Read the Key Words paragraph on page 107, and then study the map. Note the location of the **artillery** and **infantry companies,** as well as the **meadow** that is part of the battlefield. Look also at the picture on page 115. The soldier is at the ruins of an old well that contains water. Why do you suppose he is carrying so many **canteens?** How would you describe the expression on his face?

## C. Thinking About Heroic Acts

A *heroic* act is an action that is courageous, bold, noble, and admired. Think of a heroic act that you have witnessed or read about, been told about, or seen on film. What was the heroic act, and who performed it? What person (or people) in history seem to you to have been heroic? What people do you consider to be heroes in our times?

## D. Skimming to Locate and Scanning to Find Information

Sometimes we need to first *skim* a long piece of writing to find where a general topic is located, then *scan* to find information on specific details about that topic. From Exercise B, above, you already know that the subject of Crane's story is a battle during the American Civil War. You are asked now to find information about the role of horses in such a battle, and to do so quickly, without reading the whole story. Skim paragraphs 1 through 17 of the story, looking for references to horses. Then scan the paragraphs where you see such references to find answers to the following questions.

**1.** Who rode horses during Civil War battles? _____

_____

**2.** What, besides carrying riders, were horses used for in Civil War battles? _____

_____

**3.** What often happened to horses during Civil War battles?

_____

### KEY WORDS

In Crane's story, a section of the northern army, called a **regiment** (about 400 men) is fighting against an equal force of the southern army. The regiment is divided into smaller groups called **companies**. Some of these companies are **artillery**—that is, soldiers responsible for firing the largest guns, which shoot explosive **shells** that fall on the battle field like bombs. The companies of the artillery in the story are on top of a hill. Below the hill at the edge of a small field, or **meadow**, are the companies of the **infantry**—a group of soldiers who fight on foot. In the American Civil War, the soldiers of the northern army wore blue uniforms; the southern army wore gray; and infantry soldiers on both sides carried guns and metal water bottles called **canteens**.

# A MYSTERY OF HEROISM

The dark blue uniforms of the men were coated with dust from the endless struggle between the two armies. They were so dirty that the regiment almost seemed part of the clay bank which shielded the soldiers from the exploding shells.

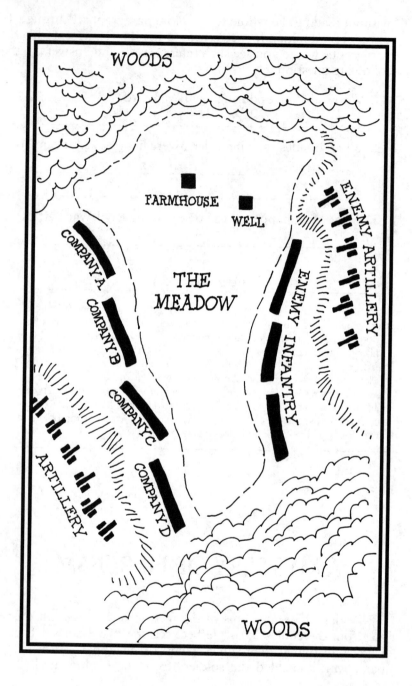

On the top of the hill the big guns were arguing in enormous roars with the enemy's guns across from them. To the eyes of the infantry soldiers below, the artillerymen, the guns, the horses, the waiting shells, were distinctly arranged against the blue sky. When a gun was fired, a huge red flash like lightning appeared low in the heavens. The artillerymen wore white trousers, which somehow emphasized their legs, and when they ran and crowded in little groups following orders from the shouting officers, they impressed the men of the infantry.

2    Fred Collins of A Company infantry was saying: "Thunder,[1] I wish I had a drink. Ain't[2] there any water around here?" Then someone yelled, "There goes the flag!"

3    As the eyes of half the regiment swept across the field in one machine-like movement, they caught the picture of a horse in a violent leap of a death. Its rider leaned back with a bent arm and fingers spread before his face. On the ground was the bright red terror of an exploding shell shooting flashes of flame. The torn flag swung clear of the rider's back as both horse and man fell forward heavily onto the ground. In the air was a smell like an enormous blazing fire.

4    Sometimes the infantry soldiers looked down at the fair little meadow which spread at their feet. Its long, green grass was rolling gently in the light wind. Beyond it was the gray form of a farmhouse half torn to pieces by shells and by the busy axes of soldiers who had used the wood for their fires. The line of an old fence was now marked by long weeds and by an occasional wooden post. A shell had blown the well-house to fragments. Little lines of smoke rose upward from the hot ashes of the place where the barn had stood.

5    From beyond a curtain of green woods there came the sound of some huge struggle, as if two animals the size of islands were fighting. At a distance there were occasional appearances of swift-moving men, horses, gun-wagons, flags. Along with the sharp crashing of infantry shots, the wild shouting and curses and cheers of men could be heard.

6    The big guns on the hill now engaged in a frightful

---

[1] thunder = the sound that follows a flash of lightning; here the word is used simply as a strong exclamation, like a curse, but without particular meaning.
[2] ain't = isn't, in nonstandard speech

exchange with the enemy's artillery. The white legs of the gunners hurried this way and that way and the officers redoubled their shouts. One of the men was suddenly hit and thrown to the ground, and his maddened companions dragged away his torn body in their struggle to escape from the confusion and danger. A young soldier on horseback cursed and shouted in his saddle³ and jerked at the straps in his hands. An officer shouted an order so violently that his voice broke and ended the sentence in a high scream.

7    The company of the infantry that was most open to danger began to move slowly toward greater protection near the hill. There was the clank of steel against steel.

8    An artillery officer rode down from the guns and passed them, holding his right arm in his left hand. And it was as if this arm was not at all a part of him, but belonged to another man. His large quiet horse moved slowly. The officer's face was grimed with dirt and wet with sweat, and his uniform was so wrinkled that it seemed he had been in a direct fight with an enemy. He smiled bitterly when the men stared at him. He turned his horse toward the meadow.

9    Collins of A Company said again:  "I wish I had a drink. I bet there's water in that old well over there!"

10    "Yes; but how're you going to get it?"

11    The little meadow that lay between the soldiers and the well was now suffering a terrible attack of shells. Its green and beautiful calm had vanished completely. Brown earth was being thrown up in monstrous handfuls. The tall young grass was being murdered—torn, burned, cut to pieces. Some curious fortune of the battle had made this gentle little meadow the object of the red hate of the shells, and each one as it exploded seemed like a horrible curse in the face of an innocent girl.

12    The wounded officer who was riding across this expanse said to himself, "Why, they couldn't shoot any harder if the whole army was gathered here!"

13    A shell struck the gray ruins of the house, and, after the explosion, the shattered wall fell in fragments, with the sound of thunder crashing sharply in a sea-storm. Indeed, the infantry, pausing in the shelter of the bank, looked like men standing upon a shore staring at the madness of a wild

---

³ saddle = a leather seat for a rider on a horse

winter ocean. The angel of disaster had turned its glance on the big guns upon the hill. Fewer white-legged men labored around them. A shell had hit one of the gun-wagons, and after the flash and smoke and dust and anger of the blow were gone, it was possible to see white legs stretched horizontally upon the ground.

14    In a space to the rear of the guns stood the artillery horses with their noses pointing at the fight. Their business was to drag the gun-wagons out of the destruction, or into it, or wherever else those strange humans demanded. Their hearts might beat wildly, but they could not forget the iron laws of man's control over them. In this line of speechless observers there had been unending and terrible destruction. From the mess of bleeding horses on the ground, the men could see one animal raising its wounded body with its forelegs and turning its nose with silent, astonishing grace toward the sky.

15    Some of his companions joked with Collins about his thirst. "Well, if you want a drink so bad, why don't you go get it?"

16    "Well, I will in a minute if you don't shut up."

17    A private in B Company, to the rear, looked out over the meadow and then turned to a companion and said, "Look there, Jim." It was the wounded officer from the infantry who had started to ride across the meadow, supporting his right arm carefully with his left hand. This man had met with a shell, apparently at a time when no one observed him. He could be seen lying face downward with one foot stretched across the body of his dead horse. One of the horse's legs extended upward precisely as stiff as an iron post. Around this motionless pair the shells still roared and howled.

18    There was a quarrel in A Company. Collins was shaking his fist in the face of some laughing companions. "Curse you! I ain't afraid to go! If you say much, I *will* go!"

19    "Of course you will! You'll run right through that there meadow, won't you?"

20    Collins said in a terrible voice: "You just watch me, now!" At this dark warning his companions broke into renewed laughter and cheers.

21    Collins gave them a dark look and went to find his captain. The captain was talking with another officer of the regiment.

22    "Captain," said Collins, standing stiffly at attention, "Captain, I want to get permission to go get some water from that well over there."

23    The captain and the other officer swung around at the same moment and stared across the meadow. The captain laughed. "You must be pretty thirsty, Collins!"

24    "Yes, sir; I am."

25    "Well—ah," said the captain. After a moment he asked: "Can't you wait?"

26    "No, sir."

27    The other officer was watching Collins's face. "Look here, my boy," he said in a serious sort of voice. "Look here, my boy." Collins was not a boy. "Don't you think that's taking big risks for a little drink of water?"

28    "I don't know," said Collins uncomfortably. Some of the anger at his companions, which perhaps had forced him into this affair, was beginning to vanish. "I don't know whether it is or not."

29    The captain and the other officer observed him for a while.

30    "Well," said the captain finally.

31    "Well," said the other officer, "If you want to go, then go."

32    Collins stood more stiffly still. "Thank you, sir!"

33    As he moved away the captain called after him, "Take some of the other boys' canteens with you and hurry back now."

34    "Yes, sir, I will."

35    The two officers looked at each other then, for it had suddenly occurred to them that they didn't know whether Collins wanted to go or not.

36    They turned to look at Collins and as they observed him surrounded by his eagerly talking companions, the captain said, "Well, by thunder! I guess he's going."

37    Collins seemed like a man dreaming. In the middle of all the questions, the advice, the warnings, all the excited talk of the men, he maintained a curious silence.

38    They were very busy preparing him for his attempt. When they inspected him carefully, it was somewhat as if

they were examining a horse before a race, and they were amazed and puzzled by the whole affair. Their astonishment was expressed in strange repetitions.

39      "Are you sure you're going?" they demanded again and again.

40      "Certainly I am," cried Collins at last, furiously.

41      He walked angrily away from them. He was swinging five or six canteens from their straps. It seemed that his hat would not remain firmly on his head, and he often reached and pulled it down over his forehead.

42      There was a general movement in the line of soldiers. The long animal-like thing moved slightly. Its four hundred eyes were turned upon the figure of Collins.

43      "Well, sir, if that ain't the damndest thing. I never thought Fred Collins had the blood in him for that kind of business."

44      "What's he going to do, anyhow?"

45      "He's going to that well there after water."

46      "We ain't dying of thirst, are we? That's foolishness."

47      "Well, somebody gave him the idea and he's doing it."

48      "Well, he must be a desperate man."

49      When Collins faced the meadow and walked away from the regiment he was half conscious that a divide, a deep valley of pride, was suddenly between him and his companions. He had blindly been led by curious emotions and had taken on a responsibility to walk squarely up to the face of death.

50      But he was not sure that he wished to take back his intention even if he could do so without shame. As a matter of truth he was sure of very little. He was mainly surprised.

51      In addition, he wondered why he did not feel some sharp pain of fear cutting his sense like a knife. He wondered at this because human expression had said loudly for centuries that men should feel afraid of certain things and that all men who did not feel this fear were very special, were heroes.

52      He was then a hero. He suffered that disappointment which we would all have if we discovered that we were ourselves capable of those brave acts which we most admire in history and legend. This, then, was a hero. In the end, heroes were not much.

53    No, it could not be true.  He could not be a hero. Heroes had no shame in their lives.  As for him, he remembered borrowing eighty dollars from a friend and promising to pay it back the next day, and then avoiding that friend for ten months.  When at home his mother had awakened him for the early work of his life on the farm, he had often been easy to anger, moody, childish, devilish, and his mother had died since he had come to the war.

54    He saw that in this matter of the well, the canteens, the shells, he was almost like a thief in the land of brave acts.

55    He was now about thirty steps from his companions. The regiment had just turned its many faces toward him. Before him was the chaos of the fight.

56    Collins suddenly felt that two devil's fingers were pressed into his ears.  He could see nothing but red arrows of flame.  He almost fell from the force of this explosion, but he made a mad rush for the house.  He viewed it as a man up to the neck in crashing waves might view the shore. In the air, little pieces of shell howled, and the earthquake explosions drove him mad with their monstrous roar.  As he ran the canteens knocked together with a rhythmical tinkling.

57    As he neared the house each detail of the scene became precise and clear.  He was aware of some bricks of the vanished chimney lying on the ground.  There was a door hanging strangely from its frame.

58    Bullets from the distant woods mixed with the shells and the pieces of shells until the air was torn in all directions by whistles, screams, howls.  When he came to the well he threw himself face downward and looked deep into its darkness.  There were hidden points of silver shining some feet from the surface.  He took one of the canteens and, unfastening its top, swung it down by the strap.  The water flowed slowly in with a lazy gurgle.

59    And now as he lay with his face turned away he was suddenly struck with the terror.  It came upon his heart and surrounded it like iron fingers.  All the power faded from his muscles.  For a moment he was no more than a dead man.

60    The canteen filled with a maddening slowness in the manner of all bottles.  Soon he recovered his strength and

directed a screaming curse at it. He leaned over until it seemed as if he intended to push water into it with his hands. He stared down into the well with eyes that shone like pieces of metal.

61    There was the nearby thunder of a shell. Red light shone through the boiling smoke and made a pink reflection on part of the wall of the well. Collins pulled out his arm and canteen as if from a hot fire. He stood up suddenly and stared and hesitated. On the ground near him lay the old bucket with a length of rusty chain. He lowered it swiftly into the well. The bucket struck the water and then, turning lazily over, sank. When he drew it out, hand reaching over shaking hand, it knocked often against the walls of the well and spilled some of its contents.

62    In running with a filled bucket, a man can use only one kind of form. So through this terrible field over which screamed the angels of death, Collins ran in the manner of a farmer chased out of the dairy by a bull.

63    His face went staring white with expectation— expectation of a blow that would throw him around and down. He would fall as he had seen other men fall, the life knocked out of them so suddenly that their knees and heads hit the ground together. He saw the long blue line of the regiment, but his companions were standing looking at him from the edge of an impossible star. He was aware of some deep wheel markings and the footprints of animals in the dirt beneath his feet.

64    The artillery officer who had fallen in this meadow had been making groans in the teeth of the storm of sound. These cries, drawn from him by his suffering, were heard only by shells and bullets. When wild-eyed Collins came running, this officer raised himself. His face wrinkled and whitened from pain, he was about to release some great begging cry. But suddenly his face straightened and he called: "Say, young man, give me a drink of water, will you?"

65    Collins had no room in his emotions for surprise. He was mad from the threats of destruction.

66    "I can't," he screamed, and in this reply was a full description of his shaking expectation. His hat was gone,

his hair stood up on end. His clothes made it appear that he had been dragged over the ground by his heels. He ran on.

67     The officer's head sank down and one elbow bent. His foot was still stretched over the body of his horse and the other leg was under it.

68     But Collins turned. He came running back. His face had now turned gray and in his eyes was all terror. "Here it is! Here it is!"

69     The officer was like a man weakened by too much drink. His arm bent like a thin branch. His head fell forward as if his neck was soft wood. He was sinking to the ground, to lie face downward.

70     Collins grabbed him by the shoulder. "Here it is. Here's your drink. Turn over! Turn over, man, for God's sake!"

71     With Collins pulling at his shoulder, the officer turned his body and fell with his face turned toward that region where the unspeakable noises of the shells lived. There was the faintest shadow of a smile on his lips as he looked at Collins. He gave a sigh, a little primitive breath like that from a child.

72     Collins tried to hold the bucket steadily, but his shaking hands caused the water to splash all over the face of the dying man. Then he grabbed it away and ran on.

73     The regiment gave him a welcoming roar. The grimed faces were wrinkled in laughter.

74     His captain waved the bucket away. "Give it to the men!"

75     Two cheerful minor officers were the first to gain possession of it. They played over it in their fashion.

76     When one tried to drink, the other playfully knocked his elbow. "Don't, Billie! You'll make me spill it," said the one. The other laughed.

77     Suddenly there was a curse, the thud of wood on the ground, and a swift murmur of astonishment from the soldiers. The two officers stared angrily at each other. The bucket lay on the ground empty.

## AFTER YOU HAVE READ THE STORY

## A. Understanding the Plot

Answer the following questions with complete sentences.

1. What armies were fighting the battle in Crane's story?
2. What had the battle done to the farmhouse in the meadow?
3. What did Fred Collins of A Company want?
4. Where was the wounded artillery officer going on his horse?
5. What did the captain and another officer give Collins permission to do?
6. Where did Collins go to get water, and what did he finally put the water in?
7. Whom did Collins meet on his way back to his company?
8. Who drank the water that Collins had risked his life to get?

## B. Understanding Words in Context

Like many words in English (and in other languages, too), the following words imitate the *sound* of the thing or action they express. Say each word out loud with a strong voice. Review its meaning in the context of the story (paragraph numbers are provided). Then complete the sentence that follows the word.

1. *howl* (17, 56)  We heard the distant howling of
   a. a cow.      b. a wolf.      c. a chickadee bird.

2. *scream* (6, 62, 66)  The instrument that can most easily be made to scream is
   a. the piano.    b. the drum.      c. the violin.

3. *clank* (7)  To get attention, the baby clanked her silver spoon against
   a. her tin cup.  b. her milk glass.   c. her mother's shoulder.

4. *tinkle* (56)  The small bell on the baby's toy tinkled
   a. because of the sunlight.
   b. because she shook it.
   c. because it was brightly painted.

5. *gurgle* (58)  A gurgle came from deep in the throat of
   a. the crying baby.
   b. the dying man.
   c. the singing opera tenor.

6. *groan* (64) She groaned loudly when
   a. the baby drank her milk.
   b. she lifted the big basket of wet clothes.
   c. her son brought home perfect grades from school.

7. *thud* (77) With a loud thud, the rock dropped straight down
   a. onto the car's windshield.
   b. into the pond.
   c. onto the bare earth.

8. *murmur* (77) The large soccer crowd began to murmur when
   a. its team scored the winning goal.
   b. the team's captain was injured.
   c. the team allowed three goals in one minute.

## C. Close Reading: "Curious Emotions"

At the center of Crane's story are the various and changing emotions that Fred Collins experiences during his extraordinary adventure. Complete the following sentences by choosing the phrase that most accurately describes Collins's state of mind at that point in the story. Paragraph numbers are given to guide your rereading.

1. The idea of going for water begins
   a. as a joke about war, and Collins decides to go in a spirit of fun.
   b. as Collins's joke about the other soldiers' thirst.
   c. as a joke about Collins's thirst, and Collins decides to go mainly because of his anger at being laughed at.
   (9–10, 15–16, 18–21)

2. When Collins asks the two officers for permission to go get water from the well,
   a. he is quite certain of himself at first but soon begins to feel unsure.
   b. he understands that they have no idea whether he really wants to go or not.
   c. he stands stiffly at attention because he fears them.
   (21–35)

3. In the minutes just before his actual departure, Collins
   a. is in a quiet, dreamlike state, but is determined to go.
   b. realizes that he is very frightened indeed.
   c. is as surprised and puzzled as the officers and other men.
   (36–42)

**4.** As Collins heads toward the meadow, "*a deep valley of pride was suddenly between him and his companions,*" but he decides that real heroes
   **a.** have no fear, and he is very afraid.
   **b.** have no shame in their lives, as he has in his.
   **c.** are not much after all, because of their fear and shame.
   (49–54)

**5.** Collins was terrified, and he knew he was terrified,
   **a.** when he felt the force of the explosion.
   **b.** as he neared the house.
   **c.** while he was slowly filling the canteen.
   (56–63)

**6.** In what is perhaps a truly heroic act, Collins
   **a.** keeps running, even though he thinks a shell or bullet might hit him.
   **b.** runs back to the wounded officer after running away from him.
   **c.** runs back to the welcoming roar of the whole regiment.
   (64–73)

## D. Vocabulary Practice

Complete the following sentences in a way that shows the meaning of the word given. Paragraph numbers are provided to help you check the word's meaning in the context of the story.

**Example:** *curse* (5, 6, 11, 18, 60) Although he tried not to use such words, he couldn't stop himself from cursing when

<u>he hit his thumb with the hammer.</u>

**1.** *fragment* (4, 13) The ancient Chinese vase was reduced to fragments when _____

_____

**2.** *vanish* (11, 28, 57) The chocolate cake seemed to vanish when _____

_____

3. *swift* (5, 61, 77)  I did my homework as swiftly as possible

   because _____

   _____

4. *grime* (8, 73)  The grime on the plate was thick, but Anna

   took care of it by _____

   _____

5. *wrinkled* (8, 64, 73)  The farmer's face was wrinkled from

   _____

   _____

6. *drag* (6, 14, 66)  She had to drag her bag of clothes down

   the hall to her room because _____

   _____

## E. Word Forms

| Noun | Verb | Adjective | Adverb |
|------|------|-----------|--------|
| impression | impress | impressive | impressively |
| emphasis | emphasize | emphatic | emphatically |
| despair, desperation | despair | desperate | desperately |
| observation | observe | observant | observantly |
| destruction | destroy | destructive | destructively |
| astonishment | astonish | astonishing, astonished | astonishingly |

Choose a word from the chart above whose form *and* meaning fit each of the following sentences.  The first one has been done for you.

1. Large shells from the artillery guns rained down all over the meadow and caused the complete **destruction** of the farmhouse.

2. "I ain't afraid to go!  If you say as much, I *will* go!" Collins declared _____.

3. The uniforms, actions, and shouts of the artillerymen were _____ to the men of the infantry.

4. Only the most _____ soldiers noticed that the wounded officer had turned his horse toward the meadow.

5. Collins _____ even himself, perhaps, by turning back to give water to the wounded officer.

6. The artillery soldiers _____ dragged their companion away from the danger of the shells exploding in front of them.

## F. Discussion: Mysteries of Heroism

1. The title of Crane's story is "A Mystery of Heroism." In your opinion, where is the mystery in Collins's act? Choose one among the possible answers below and be prepared to explain your choice.
   a. The mystery is whether Collins's act was heroic or not.
   b. The mystery is what made Collins act as he did.
   c. The mystery is why acts of courage seem meaningless in a war.
   d. The mystery is the answer to the question, "What is heroism?"
   With two or three other students who chose different answers, discuss your choice. Explain your own choice, listen to their explanations, and ask them questions about anything in their opinions that you don't understand.

2. A **symbol** is a visible thing or object used to represent something invisible, such as an idea or quality. For example, a lion is sometimes a symbol of courage; a white dove often symbolizes peace. In Crane's story, Collins, when he reaches the well, finds an old wooden bucket "*with a length of rusty chain.*" He fills this bucket with water and carries it back to his company, stopping on the way to help the wounded officer. Then, at the end of the story, "*the bucket lay on the ground empty.*" Working with a partner, find answers to the following questions and report back to the class.

- What might the bucket symbolize when Collins first finds it and fills it?
- What might it symbolize to the dying officer?
- What do you think the bucket symbolizes at the end of the story?

## G. Language Activity: A Civil War Information Search

You can find information in English about the American Civil War (1861–1865) in many different places. Choose one of the following English-language information sources to gather information on the topic suggested. Take notes as you proceed in order to make a short report to the class. Keep track of the type and amount of information provided by your source on the American Civil War. Some questions are given to guide your search, but do not limit yourself to these questions only.

1. *An English-language encyclopedia.* How many pages is the article you found under the heading "American Civil War," or "U.S. Civil War"? How many topics or subheadings does the article contain? Scan the article for names of people important in the war (generals, politicians, or others), and find which of them are the subjects of other encyclopedia articles. Under what other encyclopedia headings could you find additional information about the Civil War?

2. *An English-language library.* Using the card or computer catalog and/or the help of a librarian, find the information described in question 1.

3. *The Internet.* Using an Internet search engine (such as Yahoo!, Google, HotBot, LookSmart, etc.), find what different types or categories of information come up when you enter the search phrase "American Civil War" or "U.S. Civil War." List a number of these. Then choose one and search more deeply into it to find where it leads you.

4. *An English-speaking person who knows more than you do about the American Civil War.* Find out from this person what type of information he or she has learned about the war. Ask this person to suggest some topics about the war that you might study further (for example, the names of some people connected with the war).

## H. Writing: Fred's Narrative

Imagine you are Fred Collins. The battle is over. You are back in the army camp for a day of rest with your fellow soldiers. Tomorrow your company and regiment will start a long march to a place where you will join with many other regiments and move again to another place for another battle. Before you go, you want to write to your sister, Sarah, back home on the farm in Pennsylvania. You feel the need to tell someone about what happened on the battlefield today, and you have always been able to talk freely with Sarah. Begin your letter, "Dear Sarah."

Describe to her what happened today: what you did, why you think you did it, what you felt while you were doing it, and what the result of it was. Tell her what you are feeling about yourself right now and what your thoughts are about going into battle again soon. Ask her about the farm, and tell her what you feel about your mother's death (which she wrote you about). End your letter, "Your loving brother, Fred."

# 8

# A VISIT OF CHARITY

❋

A story by

**EUDORA WELTY**

Eudora Welty was born in 1909 in Jackson, Mississippi. She went to local schools and attended Mississippi State College for Women for two years, then finished her bachelor of arts degree at the University of Wisconsin. She also studied advertising for a year at Columbia University in New York City. She returned to Jackson after her father's death in 1931—and remained there for the rest of her long life. Welty worked for local newspapers and at the local radio station, and began writing stories. She also worked as a photographer in the Works Progress Administration, a U.S. goverment program that was formed to create jobs for people during the Great Depression of the 1930s. Her WPA collection of photographs of poor working people was published much later, in 1971, and showed her to be a fine, sympathetic photographer. She published her first collection of short stories in 1941, with an introduction by the famous author Katherine Anne Porter. The two writers remained friends and admirers of each other's work throughout their lives. Welty continued to publish novels and story collections regularly until the mid-1950s. Then, after a gap of about fifteen years, she published a novel, *The Optimist's Daughter*, which won the Pulitzer Prize. Throughout her long career, Welty wrote about the thoughts and behavior of her southern neighbors. She writes with humor and great affection about ordinary people, using dialog and carefully chosen detail to give a sense of place and character. Her sympathy with human difficulties—illness, old age, poverty, and ignorance—is clear in this story, "A Visit of Charity." Welty died in 2001.

## BEFORE YOU READ THE STORY

### A. About the Author

Read the paragraph about Eudora Welty on page 125. Where did she live most of her life? What is the location and subject of most of her writing? In addition to writing, what other creative talent did she show?

### B. The Pictures

Look at the picture on page 128. What do you think the girl is saying to the woman at the desk? What sort of building would you guess they are in? Now look at the room pictured on page 132. Do the people in the room help you decide what the building is? Did you guess correctly? To describe the furniture in this room, Welty uses some old-fashioned words that may not be familiar to you. The picture shows a closet, or **wardrobe**, for clothes. The beds are covered with a bedspread, or **counterpane**. There is a **washstand**, a small table with a water pitcher and bowl for washing. One chair is made of **wicker**, a kind of light furniture made of thin branches woven together; the other, a **rocking chair**, has bent pieces of wood under its legs so that it rocks back and forth. The floor in the rooms and hallways is covered in a kind of plastic-like covering called **linoleum**. (It is old, and in some places it no longer lies flat: it **bulges**.)

### C. Thinking About Old Age

The two old women are in a nursing home, the Old Ladies' Home, a kind of hospital for old people who cannot take care of themselves living alone. Nursing homes are common in the United States and Canada. They are not so common in many other countries. Do you come from a country where nursing homes are common? If not, how are old people cared for? Are there old people in your family? Where do they live?

### D. Scanning to Find Information

Scan the eight biographical paragraphs you have read to find information about the education received by each of these American writers. Next to each name below, enter the type or level of formal education received.

If no information is given, write **NI**. Try to complete the exercise in less than four minutes.

1. Steinbeck (p. 1)      _____
2. Hemingway (p. 15)      _____
3. Wharton (p. 29)      _____
4. Irving (p. 47)      _____
5. Hawthorne (p. 69)      _____
6. Thurber (p. 89)      _____
7. Crane (p. 105)      _____
8. Welty (p. 125)      _____

### KEY WORDS

**Charity** means good works or kindnesses done for people who are in need. The word is also used to describe agencies that organize such help. Marian, the girl in Welty's story, is a member of a girls' club, the **Campfire Girls**, who are expected to do certain charitable jobs or activities. One such job is to visit institutions in town, like the Old Ladies' Home, where people may be lonely or **ailing**—that is, not feeling well. Illness and old age are unfamiliar and frightening, or **menacing**, to Marian. The two old women she visits are not friendly to each other; they talk **spitefully** to hurt the other's feelings, and each believes the other is **contrary**—negative or difficult.

# A VISIT OF CHARITY

It was mid-morning—a very cold, bright day. Holding a potted plant before her, a girl of fourteen jumped off the bus in front of the Old Ladies' Home, on the outskirts of town. She wore a red coat, and her straight yellow hair was hanging down loose from the pointed white cap all the little girls were wearing that year. She stopped for a moment beside one of the prickly dark shrubs with which the city

had beautified the Home, and then proceeded slowly toward the building, which was of whitewashed brick and reflected the winter sunlight like a block of ice. As she walked vaguely up the steps she shifted the small pot from hand to hand; then she had to set it down and remove her mittens before she could open the heavy door.

2    "I'm a Campfire Girl. . . . I have to pay a visit to some old lady," she told the nurse at the desk. This was a woman in a white uniform who looked as if she were cold; she had close-cut hair which stood up on the very top of her head exactly like a sea wave. Marian, the little girl, did not tell her that this visit would give her a minimum of only three points in her score.

3    "Acquainted with any of our residents?" asked the nurse. She lifted one eyebrow and spoke like a man.

4    "With any old ladies? No—but—that is, any of them will do," Marian stammered. With her free hand she pushed her hair up behind her ears, as she did when it was time to study Science.

5    The nurse shrugged and rose. "You have a nice *multiflora cineraria*[1] there," she remarked as she walked ahead down the hall of closed doors to pick out an old lady.

6    There was loose, bulging linoleum on the floor. Marian felt as if she were walking on the waves, but the nurse paid no attention to it. There was a smell in the hall like the interior of a clock. Everything was silent until, behind one of the doors, an old lady of some kind cleared her throat like a sheep bleating. This decided the nurse. Stopping in her tracks, she first extended her arm, bent her elbow, and leaned forward from the hips—all to examine the watch strapped to her wrist; then she gave a loud double-rap on the door.

7    "There are two in each room," the nurse remarked over her shoulder.

8    "Two what?" asked Marian without thinking. The sound like a sheep's bleating almost made her turn around and run back.

9    One old woman was pulling the door open in short, gradual jerks, and when she saw the nurse a strange smile forced her old face dangerously awry. Marian, suddenly

---

[1] multiflora cineraria = the Latin name for a plant with bright-colored flowers, like a daisy

propelled by the strong, impatient arm of the nurse, saw next the side-face of another old woman, even older, who was lying flat in bed with a cap on and a counterpane drawn up to her chin.

10    "Visitor," said the nurse, and after one more shove she was off up the hall.

11    Marian stood tongue-tied; both hands held the potted plant. The old woman, still with that terrible, square smile (which was a smile of welcome) stamped on her bony face, was waiting. . . . Perhaps she said something. The old woman in bed said nothing at all, and she did not look around.

12    Suddenly Marian saw a hand, quick as a bird claw, reach up in the air and pluck the white cap off her head. At the same time, another claw to match drew her all the way into the room, and the next moment the door closed behind her.

13    "My, my, my," said the little old lady at her side.

14    Marian stood enclosed by the bed, a washstand and a chair; the tiny room had altogether too much furniture. Everything smelled wet—even the bare floor. She held onto the back of the chair, which was wicker and felt soft and damp. Her heart beat more and more slowly, her hands got colder and colder, and she could not hear whether the old women were saying anything or not. She could not see them very clearly. How dark it was! The window shade was down, and the only door was shut. Marian looked at the ceiling. . . . It was like being caught in a robbers' cave, just before one was murdered.

15    "Did you come to be our little girl for a while?" the first robber asked.

16    Then something was snatched from Marian's hand—the little potted plant.

17    "Flowers!" screamed the old woman. She stood holding the pot in an undecided way. "Pretty flowers," she added.

18    Then the old woman in bed cleared her throat and spoke. "They are not pretty," she said, still without looking around, but very distinctly.

19    Marian suddenly pitched against the chair and sat down in it.

20    "Pretty flowers," the first old woman insisted. "Pretty—pretty . . ."

21    Marian wished she had the little pot back for just a

moment—she had forgotten to look at the plant herself before giving it away. What did it look like?

22     "Stinkweeds,"[2] said the other old woman sharply. She had a bunchy white forehead and red eyes like a sheep. Now she turned them toward Marian. The fogginess seemed to rise in her throat again, and she bleated, "Who—are—you?"

23     To her surprise, Marian could not remember her name. "I'm a Campfire Girl," she said finally.

24     "Watch out for the germs," said the old woman like a sheep, not addressing anyone.

25     "One came out last month to see us," said the first old woman.

26     A sheep or a germ? wondered Marian dreamily, holding onto the chair.

27     "Did not!" cried the other old woman.

28     "Did so! Read to us out of the Bible, and we enjoyed it!" screamed the first.

29     "Who enjoyed it!" said the woman in the bed. Her mouth was unexpectedly small and sorrowful, like a pet's.

30     "We enjoyed it," insisted the other. "You enjoyed it—I enjoyed it."

31     "We all enjoyed it," said Marian, without realizing that she had said a word.

32     The first old woman had just finished putting the potted plant high, high on top of the wardrobe, where it could hardly be seen from below. Marian wondered how she had ever succeeded in placing it there, how she could ever have reached so high.

33     "You mustn't pay any attention to old Addie," she now said to the little girl. "She's ailing today."

34     "Will you shut your mouth?" said the woman in bed. "I am not."

35     "You're a story."[3]

36     "I can't stay but a minute—really, I can't," said Marian suddenly. She looked down at the wet floor and thought that if she were sick in here they would have to let her go.

37     With much to-do the first old woman sat down in a rocking chair—still another piece of furniture!—and began

---

[2] stinkweeds = a bad smelling wild flower that grows in wet areas
[3] you're a story = an idiom meaning "you're too much," "you're unbelievable," "you're being difficult"

to rock.  With the fingers of one hand she touched a very dirty cameo pin[4] on her chest.  "What do you do at school?" she asked.

38   "I don't know . . ." said Marian.  She tried to think but she could not.

39   "Oh, but the flowers are beautiful," the old woman whispered.  She seemed to rock faster and faster; Marian did not see how anyone could rock so fast.

40   "Ugly," said the woman in the bed.

41   "If we bring flowers . . ." Marian began, and then fell silent.  She had almost said that if Campfire Girls brought flowers to the Old Ladies' Home, the visit would count one extra point, and if they took a Bible with them on the bus and read it to the old ladies, it counted double.  But the old woman had not listened, anyway; she was rocking and watching the other one, who watched back from the bed.

42   "Poor Addie is ailing.  She has to take medicine—see?" she said, pointing a horny finger at a row of bottles on the table, and rocking so high that her black comfort shoes lifted off the floor like a little child's.

43   "I am no more sick than you are," said the woman in the bed.

44   "Oh, yes you are!"

45   "I just got more sense than you have, that's all," said the other woman, nodding her head.

46   "That's only the contrary way she talks when *you all* come," said the first old lady with sudden intimacy.  She stopped the rocker with a neat pat of her feet and leaned toward Marian.  Her hand reached over—it felt like a petunia leaf, clinging and just a little sticky.

47   "Will you hush!  Will you hush!" cried the other one.

48   Marian leaned back rigidly in her chair.

49   "When I was a little girl like you, I went to school and all," said the old woman in the same intimate, menacing voice.  "Not here—another town. . . ."

50   "Hush!" said the sick woman.  "You never went to school.  You never came and you never went.  You never were anywhere—only here.  You never were born!  You don't know anything.  Your head is empty, your heart and your hands and your old black purse are all empty, even that little old box you brought with you you brought empty—

---

[4] cameo pin = an old-fashioned piece of jewelry that has a light-colored face on a darker background

you showed it to me. And yet you talk, talk, talk, talk, talk all the time until I think I'm losing my mind! Who are you? You're a stranger—a perfect stranger! Don't you know you're a stranger? Is it possible that they have actually done a thing like this to anyone—sent them in a stranger to talk, and rock, and tell away her whole long rigmarole?[5] Do they seriously suppose that I'll be able to keep it up, day in, day out, night in, night out, living in the same room with a terrible old woman—forever?"

51     Marian saw the old woman's eyes grow bright and turn toward her. This old woman was looking at her with despair and calculation in her face. Her small lips suddenly dropped apart, and exposed a half circle of false teeth with tan gums.

52     "Come here, I want to tell you something," she whispered. "Come here!"

53     Marian was trembling, and her heart nearly stopped beating altogether for a moment.

54     "Now, now, Addie," said the first old woman. "That's not polite. Do you know what's really the matter with old Addie today?" She, too, looked at Marian; one of her eyelids drooped low.

55     "The matter?" the child repeated stupidly. "What's the matter with her?"

56     "Why, she's mad because it's her birthday!" said the first old woman, beginning to rock again and giving a little crow as though she had answered her own riddle.

57     "It is not, it is not!" screamed the old woman in bed. "It is not my birthday, no one knows when that is but myself, and will you please be quiet and say nothing more, or I'll go straight out of my mind!" She turned her eyes toward Marian again, and presently she said in a soft, foggy voice, "When the worst comes to the worst, I ring this bell, and the nurse comes." One of her hands was drawn out from under the patched counterpane—a thin little hand with enormous black freckles. With a finger which would not hold still she pointed to a little bell on the table among the bottles.

58     "How old are you?" Marian breathed. Now she could see the old woman in bed very closely and plainly, and very abruptly, from all sides, as in dreams. She wondered about

---

[5] rigmarole = a long, confused, nonsensical story

her—she wondered for a moment as though there was nothing else in the world to wonder about. It was the first time such a thing had happened to Marian.

59    "I won't tell!"

60    The old face on the pillow, where Marian was bending over it, slowly gathered and collapsed. Soft whimpers came out of the small open mouth. It was a sheep that she sounded like—a little lamb. Marian's face drew very close, the yellow hair hung forward.

61    "She's crying!" She turned a bright, burning face up to the first old woman.

62    "That's Addie for you," the old woman said spitefully.

63    Marian jumped up and moved toward the door. For the second time, the claw almost touched her hair, but it was not quick enough. The little girl put her cap on.

64    "Well, it was a real visit," said the old woman, following Marian through the doorway and all the way out into the hall. Then from behind she suddenly clutched the child with her sharp little fingers. In an affected, high-pitched whine she cried, "Oh, little girl, have you a penny to spare for a poor old woman that's got nothing of her own? We don't have a thing in the world—not a penny for candy—not a thing! Little girl, just a nickel—a penny . . ."

65    Marian pulled violently against the old hands for a moment before she was free. Then she ran down the hall, without looking behind her and without looking at the nurse, who was reading *Field & Stream*[6] at her desk. The nurse, after another triple motion to consult her wristwatch, asked automatically the question put to visitors in all institutions: "Won't you stay and have dinner with us?"

66    Marian never replied. She pushed the heavy door open into the cold air and ran down the steps.

67    Under the prickly shrub she stooped and quickly, without being seen, retrieved a red apple she had hidden there.

68    Her yellow hair under the white cap, her scarlet coat, her bare knees all flashed in the sunlight as she ran to meet the big bus rocketing through the street.

69    "Wait for me!" she shouted. As though at an imperial[7] command, the bus ground to a stop.

70    She jumped on and took a big bite out of the apple.

---

[6] *Field & Stream* = a wildlife magazine for hunters and sport fishermen
[7] imperial = as from an emperor or empress, a king or queen

## AFTER YOU READ THE STORY

### A. Understanding the Plot

Answer the following questions with complete sentences.

1. Why is Marian visiting the Old Ladies' Home?
2. How many "points" will she get toward her Campfire Girls award for her visit? In what ways could she increase this number of points?
3. How prepared is Marian for what she finds in the Old Ladies' Home?
4. How do the two old women react in their different ways to Marian's visit?
5. The two women begin to quarrel. Name at least three subjects they quarrel about.
6. What does Marian do as she runs out of the building? How does she stop the bus?

### B. Understanding Words In Context

In this exercise you are asked to guess the meaning of the <u>underlined</u> word from the **boldfaced** context clues. Sometimes there are few context clues near the word; remember to consider the story as a whole as you decide what the clues suggest. Check your answers with a dictionary.

Example: . . . *a strange smile forced her old face dangerously* <u>*awry*</u>. (9)

       <u>Awry</u> means crooked, or out of line.

1. *"With any old ladies? No—but—that is, any of them will do,"* Marian <u>stammered</u>. (4)

   *Stammered* means _____.

2. *. . . an old lady of some kind* **cleared** her **throat** *like a sheep* <u>bleating</u>. (6)

   *Bleating* means _____.

3. *Marian suddenly underline{pitched} against the chair and sat down on it.* (19)

Pitched means _____.

4. *Soft underline{whimpers} came out of the small open mouth. It was a sheep that she sounded like . . .* (60)

Whimper means _____.

5. *In an affected, high-pitched underline{whine} she cried, "Oh, little girl, have you a penny to spare for a poor old woman . . . ?"* (63)

Whine means _____.

## C. Close Reading: Marian's Experience at the Old Ladies' Home

This was Marian's first visit to a nursing home. What did she think of it? Reread these passages from the story and answer the questions that follow them.

1. *"I'm a Campfire Girl . . . . I have to pay a visit to some old lady," she told the nurse.* (2)
   *"Acquainted with any of our residents?" asked the nurse.* (3)
   *"With any old ladies? No—but—that is, any of them will do . . . "* (4)
   Does it sound as if Marian is there because she is interested in the aged? Why has she come there?

2. *"There are two in each room," the nurse remarked over her shoulder.* (7)
   *"Two what?" asked Marian without thinking.* (8)
   *Marian stood tongue-tied; both hands held the potted plant.* (11)
   How does Marian act when she first meets the two old women?

3. *Her heart beat more slowly, her hands got colder and colder, and she could not hear whether the old women were saying anything or not. . . . It was like being caught in a robbers' cave, just before one was murdered.* (14)
   What is Marian feeling now? Why?

**4.** *"If we bring flowers . . ." Marian began, and then felt silent.* (41)

What did Marian almost say? Why didn't she finish her sentence?

**5.** *Marian pulled violently against the old hands for a minute before she was free. Then she ran down the hall . . .* (65)

Why does Marian react this way?

**6.** *"Wait for me!" she shouted. As though at an imperial command, the bus ground to a stop.* (69)

What is Marian feeling at the end of the story? Why does Welty choose the word *imperial* to describe how Marian calls to the bus driver?

## D. Vocabulary Practice

Writers often use words or phrases that have *similar* but not identical meanings; this adds variety and richness to their writing. Match the word or phrase in the left column whose underlined word or phrase is most similar in meaning to an underlined word or phrase in the right column. All the words and phrases are from the story. Concentrate on the general meaning of the underlined word or phrase, not the word form. The first one has been done for you.

1. _e_ her hand . . . <u>clinging</u> and sticky (46)

    **a.** she <u>walked</u> down the hall (5)

2. ___ she <u>proceeded</u> toward the building (1)

    **b.** another claw . . . <u>drew</u> her into the room . . . (12)

3. ___ something was <u>snatched</u> from Marian's hand (16)

    **c.** she had . . . succeeded in <u>placing</u> it there (32)

4. ___ <u>propelled</u> by the . . . arm of the nurse (9)

    **d.** she saw a hand . . . <u>pluck</u> the white cap off her head (12)

5. ___ [the] old woman was <u>pulling</u> the door open (9)

    **e.** she . . . <u>clutched</u> the child with her sharp little fingers . . . (64)

6. ___ she <u>stopped in her tracks</u> (6)

    **f.** she . . . <u>leaned forward</u> from the hips (6)

7. ___ [she] . . . finished <u>putting</u> the plant . . . on top of the wardrobe (32)

g. she <u>pushed</u> the heavy door open (66)

8. ___ [she] was <u>bending</u> over [the old face] (60)

h. the bus <u>ground</u> to a stop (69)

## E. Word Forms

| Noun | Verb | Adjective |
|------|------|-----------|
| calculation | calculate | calculating, calculated |
| consultation | consul | consulting |
| extent | extend | extensive |
| intimacy | intimate | intimate |
| procedure | proceed | procedural |
| propeller, propulsion | propel | propelled |
| resident, residence | reside | residential |
| retrieval | retrieve | retrieved |

Choose the correct form of the word from the chart to complete the sentence. Then write a sentence of your own using a different form of the word. The first one is done for you.

1. *(calculate)*

    a. Yesterday I <u>**calculated**</u> that there were 225 days till my birthday.

    b. <u>**She took a calculated risk when she left her company to start her own business.**</u>

2. *(consult)*

    a. My doctor suggested that I _____ a specialist to get help with my ailing back.

    b. _____

**3.** *(extend)*

    **a.** The Spanish teacher's _____ travel experience was clear to her students—she had been all over South America

    **b.** _____

**4.** *(intimate)*

    **a.** We had known them for many years, but we didn't share the kind of _____ that made it easy to describe our problems to them.

    **b.** _____

**5.** *(proceed)*

    **a.** After the lecture, the students _____ to ask questions.

    **b.** _____

**6.** *(propel)*

    **a.** The crew had to repair the plane's _____ before it could take off.

    **b.** _____

**7.** *(reside)*

    **a.** My grandfather moved to a seniors' _____ when he became too old to live by himself.

    **b.** _____

**8.** *(retrieve)*

    **a.** The soccer player _____ the ball from inside the goal.

    **b.** _____

## F. Discussion: Charity Work

Most parents and teachers, as well as social organizations like churches and youth clubs, encourage young people to develop an interest in charitable work. They believe that we are all capable of learning to help others and that by helping the less fortunate we become better people ourselves. Do you agree with this? Why, or why not? Do you think Marian learned something from her visit to the Old Ladies' Home? What did she learn? Have you ever been in an organization that encouraged its members to do good works? What did you do? Were you successful? Why, or why not? Could you do better in the future? How?

## G. Language Activity: Project on Aging

Aging is a natural, normal part of life—it happens to everyone who lives long enough. Divide into small groups to study questions related to aging. Choose one of the topics below to research, and report to the class.

1. If you are living in the United States or Canada:
   a. In the United States and Canada, many elderly people live in some sort of residential house or institution, not their own home. Using the sources of information listed in Exercise G on pages 13 and 123, find out what different types of residential homes or institutions exist near you. For search words or phrases, use one or more of the following: Council on Aging, assisted living, rest homes, nursing homes.
   b. A number of organizations exist to help with the interests and concerns of the aging, such as the American Association of Retired People (AARP) and the Canadian Association of Retired Persons (CARP). To find out what they offer, contact the AARP at 601 E St. NW, Washington, D.C. 20049, or at their website, www.aarp.org, or contact the CARP at Suite 1304, 27 Queen St. E, Toronto, ON, M5C 2M6, or at their website, www.50plus.com. What other organizations can you find that deal with the aged, and what do they do?

**2.** If you are living outside North America:
Find an English-language information source—library,
bookstore, information agency, consulate, Internet—and
collect information about resources for aging people that
might be useful to older people in general.

## H. Writing: Compare and Contrast

In this exercise, you are asked to compare "A Visit of Charity"
with either "April Showers," by Edith Wharton, or "A Day's
Wait," by Ernest Hemingway. Write at least three paragraphs,
about 200 words, describing the similarities and differences in
the two stories, and what you liked and didn't like about both.
Consider the following as you write: the characters and what
they learned or didn't learn about themselves and others, and
the tone of voice the authors use to describe the situation
(humor? sadness? realism?). What was your reaction as you
read the stories? After you had finished the stories?

# 9

# THE BLACK BALL

✳

A story by

**RALPH ELLISON**

Ralph Waldo Ellison was born in Oklahoma City, Oklahoma, in 1914. His parents had moved there from the deep South not long after Oklahoma became a state. Like other African-Americans, the Ellisons were attracted to Oklahoma because the new state had no strong tradition of slavery, and a life of greater equality with whites seemed possible. Ellison's father died when he was three, and the family suffered hard times. Ellison's mother was committed to education and political activism, however, and encouraged Ralph and his brother to read widely. Ellison received a scholarship to study music at Tuskeegee Institute, a college for African-American students in Alabama. After two years at Tuskeegee, he went to New York City to find a summer job, and never returned to the South. In New York he met Richard Wright, an African-American writer and political activist, who encouraged him to write. Ellison served in the Merchant Marine during World War II. Then, in 1952, he published the novel *Invisible Man*, which became an immediate success. *Invisible Man* illustrated the nature of race relations in the United States and was very influential during a time of great change in the country. The title, *Invisible Man*, suggests the theme of Ellison's writing: the lack of worth of black people in the eyes of the white world. The novel won the National Book Award in 1953. Identity, race, and racism are Ellison's continuing concerns. Most of his stories, like "The Black Ball," show a young black man who gains awareness of his cultural, racial, and social identity. Ellison taught at several universities and published many critical essays, later collected in book form. A second novel was lost in a house fire, and painfully rewritten. It and his collected short stories were not published until after his death in 1994, in New York City.

# BEFORE YOU READ THE STORY

## A. About the Author

Read the paragraph about Ralph Ellison on page 143. Why did his parents think that Oklahoma would be a good state to live in? What did Ellison originally plan to study in college? What are Ellison's central concerns as a writer?

## B. The Pictures

Three men are in the picture on page 151: a black man (right), a white man wearing a **derby** hat and carrying a walking **stick** (left), and another white man (center, walking toward us). What type of work would you guess each man does? In the picture on page 155, a father and son are looking up at a man (the man with the derby hat in the first picture) standing at a window. Why might the man be holding a ball? Why might the boy be crying?

## C. Thinking About Race and Racism

As the biographical paragraph on page 143 tells us, "identity, race, and racism are Ellison's continuing concerns." If you are not familiar with the word "racism," look it up in your dictionary. Have you personally experienced or seen an act of racism? Where did it occur? How did it make you feel? What action, if any, did you take as a result of it?

## D. Skimming and Scanning for What Interests You

Imagine you have been asked to choose one author of the nine in this book as a subject for further study. Skim the nine biographical paragraphs about the authors to refresh your memory, scanning as you go for details of the authors' lives that you find particularly interesting. Then answer the following three questions.

1. Which of these nine people would you choose for further study?
2. What aspect of his or her life do you find particularly interesting? Examples might include: childhood, education, travels, family life, literary achievements, writing style, professional experiences, personality, and so on.

3. What aspect of a person's life *not* mentioned in the biographical paragraph would you be interested in learning more about?

## KEY WORDS

The story's title, **"The Black Ball**," refers to the table game of pool, which is played with a long stick called a **cue** and small, hard, colored balls. One of these balls, the "eight ball," is black and, if played incorrectly, can make a player lose quickly. The idiomatic phrase "behind the black ball (or behind the eight ball)" means "in a dangerous or losing situation." One of the main characters in the story works for a labor **union**—an organization formed to help protect the rights, interests, and financial security of working people.

Several words that refer to **African-Americans** appear in Ellison's story. In the United States, **negro** was the formal term for African-Americans commonly used into the first half of the twentieth century; it was replaced in the second half of the century by the term **black** American, or the more formal **African-American**. **Colored** was another less formal term used for all nonwhite people in the United States and elsewhere. **People of color** is now the current formal term for nonwhite people. **Nigger** was and is an extremely impolite, insulting, racist word.

# THE BLACK BALL

I had rushed through the early part of the day mopping the lobby, placing fresh sand in the tall green jars, sweeping and dusting the halls, and emptying the trash to be burned later on in the day into the incinerator. And I had stopped only once to chase out after a can of milk for Mrs. Johnson, who had a new baby and who was always nice to my boy. I had started at six o'clock, and around eight I ran out to the quarters where we lived over the garage to dress the boy and give him his fruit and cereal. He was very thoughtful sitting there in his high chair and paused several times with his spoon midway to his mouth to watch me as I chewed my toast.

2    "What's the matter, son?"

3    "Daddy, am I black?

4    "Of course not, you're brown. You know you're not black."

5    "Well yesterday Jackie said I was so black."

6    "He was just kidding. You mustn't let them kid you, son."

7    "Brown's much nicer than white, isn't it, Daddy?"

8    He was four, a little brown boy in rompers,[1] and when he talked and laughed with imaginary playmates, his voice was soft and round in its accents like those of most Negro Americans.

9    "Some people think so. But American is better than both, son."

10   "Is it, Daddy?"

11   "Sure it is. Now forget this talk about you being black, and Daddy will be back as soon as he finishes his work."

12   I left him to play with his toys and a book of pictures until I returned. He was a pretty nice fellow, as he used to say after particularly quiet afternoons while I tried to study, and for which quietness he expected a treat of candy or a "picture movie," and I often let him alone while I attended to my duties in the apartments.

13   I had gone back and started doing the brass[2] on the front doors when a fellow came up and stood watching from the street. He was lean and red in the face with that redness that comes from a long diet of certain foods. You see much of it in the deep South, and here in the Southwest it is not uncommon. He stood there watching, and I could feel his eyes in my back as I polished the brass.

14   I gave special attention to that brass because for Berry, the manager, the luster of these brass panels and door handles was a measure of all my industry. It was near time for him to arrive.

15   "Good morning, John," he would say, looking not at me but at the brass.

16   "Good morning, sir," I would say, looking not at him but at the brass. Usually his face was reflected there. Besides that brass, his money, and the half-dozen or so

---

[1] rompers = a type of one-piece clothing for small children
[2] brass = shiny, gold-colored metal

plants in his office, I don't believe he had any other real interests in life.

17      There must be no flaws this morning. Two fellows who worked at the building across the street had already been dismissed because whites had demanded their jobs, and with the boy at that age needing special foods and me planning to enter school again next term, I couldn't afford to allow something like that out on the sidewalk to spoil my chances. Especially since Berry had told one of my friends in the building that he didn't like that "damned educated nigger."

18      I was so concerned with the brass that when the fellow spoke, I jumped with surprise.

19      "Howdy,"[3] he said.   The expected drawl[4] was there. But something was missing, something usually behind that kind of drawl.

20      "Good morning."

21      "Looks like you working pretty hard over that brass."

22      "It gets pretty dirty overnight."

23      That part wasn't missing.   When they did have something to say to us, they always became familiar.

24      "You been working here long?" he asked, leaning against the column with his elbow.

25      "Two months."

26      I turned my back to him as I worked.

27      "Any other colored folks working here?"

28      "I'm the only one," I lied.  There were two others.  It was none of his business anyway.

29      "Have much to do?"

30      "I have enough," I said.  Why, I thought, doesn't he go on in and ask for the job? Why bother me? Why tempt me to choke him? Doesn't he know we aren't afraid to fight his kind out this way?

31      As I turned, picking up the bottle to pour more polish on my rag, he pulled a tobacco sack from the pocket of his old blue coat.  I noticed his hands were scarred as though they had been burned.

32      "Ever smoke Durham?" he asked.

33      "No thank you," I said.

34      He laughed.

35      "Not used to anything like that, are you?"

---

[3] howdy = an informal word for *hello*
[4] drawl = speech with a slow, lengthened tone, associated with the deep South of the United States

36      "Not used to what?"

37      A little more from this guy and I would see red.

38      "Fellow like me offering a fellow like you something besides a rope."

39      I stopped to look at him. He stood there smiling with the sack in his outstretched hand. There were many wrinkles around his eyes, and I had to smile in return. In spite of myself I had to smile.

40      "Sure you won't smoke some Durham?"

41      "No thanks," I said.

42      He was fooled by the smile. A smile couldn't change things between my kind and his.

43      "I'll admit it ain't much," he said. "But it's a helluva lot different."

44      I stopped the polishing again to see what it was he was trying to get after.

45      "But," he said, "I've got something really worth a lot; that is, if you're interested."

46      "Let's hear it," I said.

47      Here, I thought, is where he tries to put something over on old "George."

48      "You see, I come out from the union and we intend to organize all the building-service help in this district. Maybe you been reading about it in the papers?"

49      "I saw something about it, but what's it to do with me?"

50      "Well, first place we'll make 'em take some of this work off you. It'll mean shorter hours and higher wages, and better conditions in general."

51      "What you really mean is that you'll get in here and bounce me out. Unions don't want Negro members."

52      "You mean *some* unions don't. It used to be that way, but things have changed."

53      "Listen, fellow. You're wasting your time and mine. Your damn unions are like everything else in the county— for whites only. What ever caused *you* to give a damn about a Negro anyway? Why should *you* try to organize Negroes?"

54      His face had become a little white.

55      "See them hands?"

56      He stretched out his hands.

57      "Yes," I said, looking not at his hands but at the color draining from his face.

58      "Well, I got them scars in Macon County, Alabama, for

saying a colored friend of mine was somewhere else on a day he was supposed to have raped[5] a woman. He was, too, 'cause I was with him. Me and him was trying to borrow some seed fifty miles away when it happened—if it did happen. They made them scars with a gasoline torch and run me out of the county 'cause they said I tried to help a nigger make a white woman out a lie.[6] That same night they lynched[7] him and burned down his house. They did that to him and this to me, and both of us was fifty miles away."

59    He was looking down at his outstretched hands as he talked.

60    "God," was all I could say. I felt terrible when I looked closely at his hands for the first time. It must have been hell. The skin was drawn and puckered and looked as though it had been fried. Fried hands.

61    "Since that time I learned a lot," he said. "I been at this kinda thing. First it was the croppers,[8] and when they got to know me and made it too hot, I quit the county and came to town. First it was in Arkansas and now it's here. And the more I move around, the more I see, and the more I see, the more I work."

62    He was looking into my face now, his eyes blue in his red skin. He was looking very earnestly. I said nothing. I didn't know what to say to that. Perhaps he was telling the truth; I didn't know. He was smiling again.

63    "Listen," he said. "Now, don't you go trying to figger it all out right now. There's going to be a series of meetings at this number starting tonight, and I'd like mighty much to see you there. Bring any friends along you want to."

64    He handed me a card with a number and 8 P.M. sharp written on it. He smiled as I took the card and made as if to shake my hand but turned and walked down the steps to the street. I noticed that he limped as he moved away.

65    "Good morning, John," Mr. Berry said. I turned, and there he stood; derby, long black coat, stick, nose glasses, and all. He stood gazing into the brass like the wicked

---

[5] raped = forced a sexual act upon
[6] make a white woman out a lie = make it seem as if a white woman told a lie
[7] lynched = hanged, illegally, by a rope until dead
[8] croppers = farm workers who work on someone else's large farm and receive part of the crop as wages

queen into her looking glass in the story which the boy liked so well.[9]

66     "Good morning, sir," I said.

67     I should have finished long before.

68     "Did the man I saw leaving wish to see me, John?"

69     "Oh no, sir. He only wished to buy old clothes."

70     Satisfied with my work for the day, he passed inside, and I walked around to the quarters to look after the boy. It was near twelve o'clock.

71     I found the boy pushing a toy back and forth beneath a chair in the little room which I used for a study.

72     "Hi, Daddy," he called.

73     "Hi, son," I called. "What are you doing today?"

74     "Oh, I'm trucking."[10]

75     "I thought you had to stand up to truck."

76     "Not that kind, Daddy, this kind."

77     He held up the toy.

78     "Ooh," I said. "*That* kind."

79     "Aw, Daddy, you're kidding. You always kid, don't you, Daddy?"

80     "No. When you're bad I don't kid, do I?"

81     "I guess not."

82     In fact, he wasn't bad—only enough to make it unnecessary for me to worry because he wasn't.

83     The business of trucking soon absorbed him, and I went back to the kitchen to fix his lunch and to warm up the coffee for myself.

84     The boy had a good appetite, so I didn't have to make him eat. I gave him his food and settled into a chair to study, but my mind wandered away, so I got up and filled a pipe hoping that would help, but it didn't, so I threw the book aside and picked up Malraux's *Man's Fate*, which Mrs. Johnson had given me, and tried to read it as I drank a cup of coffee. I had to give that up also. Those hands were on my brain, and I couldn't forget that fellow.

85     "Daddy," the boy called softly; it's always softly when I'm busy.

86     "Yes, son."

87     "When I grow up I think I'll drive a truck."

---

[9] the story that the boy liked so well = a fairy tale, "Snow White and the Seven Dwarfs"
[10] trucking = moving something with a truck, or pulling or pushing a load with a hand truck—a small platform on wheels

88  "You do?"

89  "Yes, and then I can wear a lot of buttons on my cap like the men that bring the meat to the grocery. I saw a colored man with some today, Daddy. I looked out the window, and a colored man drove the truck today, and, Daddy, he had two buttons on his cap. I could see 'em plain."

90  He had stopped his play and was still on his knees, beside the chair in his blue overalls. I closed the book and looked at the boy a long time. I must have looked queer.

91  "What's the matter, Daddy?" he asked. I explained that I was thinking, and got up and walked over to stand looking out the front window. He was quiet for a while; then he started rolling his truck again.

92  The only nice feature about the quarters was that they were high up and offered a view in all directions. It was afternoon and the sun was brilliant. Off to the side, a boy and girl were playing tennis in a driveway. Across the street a group of little fellows in bright sunsuits were playing on a long stretch of lawn before a white stone building. Their nurse, dressed completely in white except for her dark glasses, which I saw when she raised her head, sat still as a picture, bent over a book on her knees. As the children played, the wind blew their cries over to where I stood, and as I watched, a flock of pigeons swooped down into the driveway near the stretch of green, only to take flight again wheeling in a mass as another child came skipping up the drive pulling some sort of toy. The children saw him and were running toward him in a group when the nurse looked up and called them back. She called something to the child and pointed back in the direction of the garages where he had just come from. I could see him turn slowly around and drag his toy, some kind of bird that flapped its wings like an eagle, slowly after him. He stopped and pulled a flower from one of the bushes that lined the drive, turning to look hurriedly at the nurse, and then ran back down the drive. The child had been Jackie, the little son of the white gardener who worked across the street.

93  As I turned away I noticed that my boy had come to stand beside me.

94  "What are you looking at, Daddy?"

95  "I guess Daddy was just looking out on the world."

96    Then he asked if he could go out and play with his ball, and since I would soon have to go down myself to water the lawn, I told him it would be all right. But he couldn't find the ball; I would have to find it for him.

97    "All right now," I told him. "You stay in the back out of everybody's way, and you mustn't ask anyone a lot of questions."

98    I always warned about the questions, even though it did little good. He ran down the stairs, and soon I could hear the *bump bump bump* of his ball bouncing against the garage doors underneath. But since it didn't make a loud noise, I didn't ask him to stop.

99    I picked up the book to read again, and must have fallen asleep immediately, for when I came to it was almost time to go water the lawn. When I got downstairs, the boy was not there. I called, but no answer. Then I went out into the alley in back of the garage to see if he was playing there. There were three older white boys sitting talking on a pile of old packing cases. They looked uneasy when I came up. I asked if they had seen a little Negro boy, but they said they hadn't. Then I went further down the alley behind the grocery store where the trucks drove up, and asked one of the fellows working there if he had seen my boy. He said he had been working on the platform all afternoon and that he was sure the boy had not been there. As I started away, the four o'clock whistle blew and I had to go water the lawn. I wondered where the boy could have gone. As I came back up the alley I was becoming alarmed. Then it occurred to me that he might have gone out in front in spite of my warning not to. Of course, that is where he would go, out in front to sit on the grass. I laughed at myself for becoming alarmed and decided not to punish him, even though Berry had given instructions that he was not to be seen out in front without me. A boy that size will make you do that.

100   As I came around the building past the tall new evergreens, I could hear the boy crying in just that note no other child has, and when I came completely around I found him standing looking up into a window with tears on his face.

101   "What is it, son?" I asked. "What happened?"

102   "My ball, my ball, Daddy. My ball," he cried, looking up at the window.

103    "Yes, son, but what about the ball?"

104    "He threw it up in the window."

105    "Who did? Who threw it, son? Stop crying and tell Daddy about it."

106    He made an effort to stop, wiping the tears away with the back of his hand.

107    "A big white boy asked me to throw him my ball an', an' he took it and threw it up in that window and ran," he said, pointing.

108    I looked up just as Berry appeared at the window. The ball had gone into his private office.

109    "John, is that your boy?" he snapped.

110    He was red in the face.

111    "Yessir, but—"

112    "Well, he's taken his damned ball and ruined one of my plants."

113    "Yessir."

114    "You know he's got no business around here in front, don't you?"

115    "Yes!"

116    "Well, if I ever see him around here again, you're going to find yourself behind the black ball. Now get him on round to the back and then come up here and clean up this mess he's made."

117    I gave him one long hard look and then felt for the boy's hand to take him back to the quarters. I had a hard time seeing as we walked back, and scratched myself by stumbling into the evergreens as we went around the building.

118    The boy was not crying now, and when I looked down at him, the pain in my hand caused me to notice that it was bleeding. When we got upstairs, I sat the boy in a chair and went looking for iodine to doctor my hand.

119    "If anyone should ask me, young man, I'd say your face needed a good washing."

120    He didn't answer then, but when I came out of the bathroom, he seemed more inclined to talk.

121    "Daddy, what did that man mean?"

122    "Mean how, son?"

123    "About a black ball. You know, Daddy."

124    "Oh—that."

125    "You know, Daddy. What'd he mean?"

126    "He meant, son, that if your ball landed in his office again, Daddy would go after it behind the old black ball."

127    "Oh," he said, very thoughtful again. Then, after a while he told me: "Daddy, that white man can't see very good, can he, Daddy?"

128    "Why do you say that, son?"

129    "Daddy," he said impatiently. "Anybody can see my ball is white."

130    For the second time that day I looked at him a long time.

131    "Yes, son," I said. "Your ball *is* white." Mostly white, anyway, I thought.

132    "Will I play with the black ball, Daddy?"

133    "In time, son," I said. "In time."

134    He had already played with the ball; that he would discover later. He was learning the rules of the game already, but he didn't know it. Yes, he would play with the ball. Indeed, poor little rascal,[11] he would play until he grew sick of playing. My, yes, the old ball game. But I'd begin teaching him the rules later.

135    My hand was still burning from the scratch as I dragged the hose out to water the lawn, and looking down at the iodine stain, I thought of the fellow's fried hands, and felt in my pocket to make sure I still had the card he had given me. Maybe there was a color other than white on the old ball.

---

[11] rascal: used about children = affectionate word meaning something like "little devil"; used about adults = a tricky or dishonest person.

# AFTER YOU READ THE STORY

## A. Understanding the Plot

Answer the following questions with complete sentences.

1. Where do John and his son live? What is John's job? (Did you guess correctly in Exercise B on page 144?)
2. What three things does John's boss, Mr. Berry, seem to care most about?
3. Why is John so careful to make no mistakes in his work?
4. Why does the red-faced man want to talk with John, and what is John's response?
5. How did the union man get the scars on his hands? Why did he get them?
6. What happens to the boy's ball, and what is the result of this incident?
7. Why, at the end of the story, does John feel in his pocket to make sure he has the card that the other man gave him?

## B. Understanding Words in Context

The narrator of "The Black Ball" tells his story using educated but informal and idiomatic English. The union organizer (the man with the scarred hands) uses many nonstandard expressions. While these various idioms and other expressions may be new to you, most can be understood with a little thought about the context. For each underlined word or phrase from the story below, write a definition, synonym, or explanation of its meaning in the space provided. The paragraph number is given so that you can review the full context.

1. The narrator's informal and idiomatic expressions:

   a. . . . *I had stopped only once <u>to chase out after</u> a can of milk for Mrs. Johnson . . .* (1)

   _____

   b. *I had gone back and started <u>doing</u> the brass . . .* (13)

   _____

c. *A little more from this guy and I would <u>see red</u>.* (37)

_____

d. *I stopped the polishing again to see what it was he was trying to <u>get after</u>.* (44)

_____

e. *"What you really mean is that you'll get in here and <u>bounce me out</u> . . . ."* (51)

_____

f. *"What ever caused you to <u>give a damn about</u> a Negro anyway? . . ."* (53)

_____

2. The union organizer's nonstandard expressions. (Write the standard spelling or grammatical structure in the space provided. The first one is done for you.)

a. *". . . Looks like <u>you working pretty hard</u> . . ."* (21)

**you're working pretty hard**

b. *"<u>You been working</u> here long?"* (24)

_____

c. *". . . it ain't much. . . . But it's <u>a helluva lot</u> different."* (43)

_____

d. *"See <u>them hands?</u>"* (55)

_____

e. *"<u>Me and him was</u> trying to borrow some seed . . ."* (58)

_____

f. *"<u>I been</u> at this <u>kinda</u> thing."* (61)

_____

g. *"Now don't you <u>go trying to figger</u> it all out . . ."* (63)

_____

# C. Close Reading: Implied Meaning

Sometimes Ellison shows us his characters' opinions and attitudes by implying rather than clearly stating them. Read the indicated paragraphs again and answer the questions about the implied meaning in them.

1. John and the union organizer:
   a. Paragraph 17: What is John referring to in the phrase *"something like that out on the sidewalk"*? What could "that" mean?
   b. Paragraphs 19–23: When John says *"something was missing"* in the white man's way of talking, what does he mean? What tone of voice does he expect from men who look like that white man?
   c. Paragraphs 32–39: What does the phrase *"offering . . . a rope"* mean here? (Hint: See footnote 7 on page 149.) Why does John smile at this comment, in spite of himself?
   d. Paragraphs 39–42: When John tells us that *"a smile couldn't change things between my kind and his,"* what does he mean by "my kind" and what does he mean by "his [kind]"? What are the "things" that he thinks can't be changed?

2. John and Mr. Berry:
   a. Paragraphs 116–117: After Berry tells John to keep his son in back of the building, John says he *"had a hard time seeing"* as he and the boy walked back. What does he mean by this?
   b. Paragraphs 127–134: What does John mean when he says that his son *"had already played with the ball; that he would discover later"*? What is "the ball" here? Why doesn't the boy know he has already played with it?
   c. Paragraphs 134–135: John thinks to himself, *"My, yes, the old ball game. But I'd begin teaching him the rules later."* What do you think some of these rules might be?

## D. Vocabulary Practice

Several words in "The Black Ball" refer to John's job as the caretaker of an apartment building. Match the words in the left column with the correct definition in the right column. Then write your own sentence that shows the meaning of each word. The first one has been done for you.

1. _c_ mop      **a.** a container for burning things

2. ___ rag      **b.** a flexible pipe made of rubber or soft plastic, through which water flows

3. ___ trash      **c.** a tool used for cleaning floors with water and soap

4. ___ incinerator      **d.** a place to live

5. ___ lobby      **e.** worn, broken, or worthless things

6. ___ quarters      **f.** a cloth used for cleaning or polishing

7. ___ hose      **g.** the entrance hallway of a large building

1. *(mop)* I wet the mop with soapy water from the pail and began to clean the kitchen floor.

2. *(rag)* _____

_____

3. *(trash)* _____

_____

4. *(incinerator)* _____

_____

5. *(lobby)* _____

_____

6. *(quarters)* _____

_____

7. *(hose)* _____

_____

## E. Word Forms

| Noun | Verb | Adjective | Adverb |
|---|---|---|---|
| dismissal | dismiss | dismissive | dismissively |
| inclination, incline | incline | inclining, inclined | |
| absorption | absorb | absorbing, absorbed | absorbingly |
| kidder | kid | kidding, kidded | kiddingly |
| stumble | stumble | stumbling | stumblingly |
| quitter | quit | quitting | |
| temptation | tempt | tempting | temptingly |

Put the correct form of the italicized word into the space provided, then complete the sentence in a way that demonstrates the word's meaning.

1. (quit) "It's _____ time!" he shouted, and all the workers _____.

2. (dismiss) Rob's _____ from college shocked his parents because _____.

3. (incline) Her _____ was to trust him despite _____.

4. (absorb) My mother found the book so _____ that she _____.

5. (kid) The baby is eating spinach? You're _____ me. I thought _____.

6. (stumble) He _____ over his words because _____.

7. (tempt) Chocolate candy is a great _____ for me, even though _____.

## F. Discussion: Race and Social Class

1. What does John mean when he tells his son that "American" is better than "brown or white"? (paragraphs 2–9) Why does he feel he needs to say this to the child? Which of the other two adult characters in the story do you think might share his attitude? Why?

2. In paragraph 92, a child (a boy) approaches some other children, who run toward him, eager to join him and play with him. But the children's nurse calls them back and sends the other boy away. All the children are white, so this is not an act of racism. What is it, then? Is this a matter of social class? What makes the little boy "different from" (and in the nurse's opinion "inferior to") the other children?

3. What do you think Berry's opinion of the union man would be if he saw him in the street (and knew nothing about his work)? What standards would Berry use to form his opinion? In this sense, how are Berry and the nurse similar?

## G. Language Activity: Further Study

In Exercise D on page 144, you were asked to choose one author from the nine in this book as a subject for further study. Also, you were asked to think about one particular aspect of the author's life that you would be interested in learning more about. Using your choices there (or making new ones), and using one or more of the sources of information suggested in Exercise G on pages 13 and 123, find information about the aspect of the life of the author you have chosen (review again the short list of topics in question 2 in Exercise D on page 144). Remember that the aspect you choose may be one that does not appear in the biographical paragraph in this book. Take notes during your information search. Prepare a brief (one- to two-minute) report to the class on your topic, and be aware, as you progress in your research, that you will be asked to write a report on what you find in Exercise H on page 163.

## H. Writing: A Biographical Essay

Write an essay of 300–500 words on the author and topic you researched for Exercise G on page 162. Although you do not need to limit yourself to three paragraphs, you should cover the following topics in your essay.

- Introduce the author and the particular aspect of his or her life that you chose to focus on.
- Report in some detail on the aspect you have chosen.
- Relate the aspect you have chosen to the author's career as a writer, or to a theme in his or her literary work, or to his or her personality or personal philosophy, showing why the aspect you have chosen was particularly important to the author's work.

# ANSWER KEY

Note: Generally, no answers are given to questions that ask for the reader's opinion. But sample answers are given for some exercises in which the student is asked to use his or her own words.

## 1. BREAKFAST

### BEFORE YOU READ THE STORY

#### A. About the Author

Many of Steinbeck's stories are set in the farming valley where he grew up. Steinbeck's jobs developed in him a deep sympathy for working people.

#### B. The Picture

In the picture are: iron stove, packing box, tin cups, dungarees, biscuits.

#### D. Scanning for Information

1. The words or phrases that come just before or after it.
2. The context helps you understand the new word's meaning.
3. Context clues are the words and phrases that point to, and help you understand, the meaning of a new word.
4. **iron stove:** "for cooking"; **packing box:** "used as a table"; **tin cups:** "and plates"; **picking cotton:** "taking cotton off the plant by hand"; **dungarees:** "clothing made of rough dark-blue cotton (blue jeans)"; **biscuits:** "quickly made bread baked in a pan in small round shapes"

### AFTER YOU READ THE STORY

#### A. Understanding the Plot

1. It was very early in the morning. It was cold.
2. He saw a tent, an orange fire, and an old rusty iron stove.

3. The woman was working at the stove, making breakfast. Her baby was with her as she worked.
4. The two men were dressed in new blue dungaree pants and coats. They were both sharp-faced men.
5. They had been picking cotton.
6. They had bacon, biscuits, gravy, and coffee for breakfast.
7. The younger man invited the narrator to pick cotton with them. The narrator said "No."
8. The narrator feels a rush of warmth when he thinks of it.

## B. Understanding Words in Context

1. b   3. b   5. a   7. c
2. c   4. a   6. b   8. b

## C. Close Reading: Simplicity

1. "the light, quick gracefulness of her movements," "there was something very precise and practiced in her movements."
2. The older man said, "God Almighty, it's good," and he filled his mouth again. They all ate quickly and frantically until they were full and warm.
3. He came near to the stove to warm himself, and waited till they spoke to him.
4. His face was neither friendly nor unfriendly.
5. They were wearing new dungaree pants and coats. "They both smiled a little" when they looked at their new dungarees. They were happy about them.
6. The narrator saw "the image of the mountain and the light coming over it reflected in the older man's eyes."

## D. Vocabulary Practice

1. shiver    3. averted       5. sunken      7. swiftly
2. recall    4. gracefulness  6. dissipate   8. spurted

## E. Word Forms

1. flashing   3. rushed     5. stretched
2. gleaming   4. shivering

# 2. A DAY'S WAIT

## BEFORE YOU READ THE STORY

### A. About the Author

Hemingway served as a Red Cross ambulance driver in World War I and was seriously wounded. He had a clean, clear writing style.

### B. The Pictures

The boy looks sick, and there are pills on the table next to the bed. It is winter.

### D. Scanning Two Sources of Information

1. Steinbeck lived the longest.
2. Steinbeck set his stories in Salinas, California. Hemingway set his stories in Europe.
3. Steinbeck often wrote about working people (farming families). Hemingway often wrote about war.
4. Both writers have a clean, clear, natural writing style.
5. Both writers won the Nobel Prize for literature.

## AFTER YOU READ THE STORY

### A. Understanding the Plot

1. The boy was shivering, his face was white, and he walked slowly.
2. The boy's temperature was one hundred and two.
3. The doctor told the father there was nothing to worry about if the fever did not go above one hundred and four degrees.
4. He lay still in the bed and seemed very detached from what was going on. The boy did not follow what the father was reading.

5. He did not think the boy's condition was very serious.
6. The boy thought he was going to die.
7. The boy understood that he had been mistaken about how serious his temperature was.
8. The boy's hold over himself was slack, and he cried easily at things that were of no importance.

## B. Understanding Words in Context

1. a.   2. b   3. b   4. c   5. a

## C. Close Reading: Clues to Character

1. T
2. F  The boy is afraid to go to sleep.
3. F  The boy means his death.
4. T

## D. Vocabulary Practice

| | | |
|---|---|---|
| 1. temperature | 4. shiver | 7. pneumonia |
| 2. thermometer | 5. ache | 8. prescription |
| 3. fever | 6. influenza | 9. epidemic |

## E. Word Forms

commence
detachment
poised
prescribe
relaxed

| | | |
|---|---|---|
| 1. relaxation | 3. prescribed | 5. poised |
| 2. commencement | 4. detachment | |

# 3. APRIL SHOWERS

### A. About the Author

Wharton was taught at home by governesses. She lived in France for most of her adult life. She usually wrote about upper-class New York society people.

### B. The Pictures

The young woman is standing in a garden. It is spring. It is night. She holds a letter in her hand. She looks happy. She is in an office. She looks unhappy.

### D. Skimming to Get an Impression

1. She seems to be young—probably a teenager.
2. It seems to take place at the girl's home.
3. Uncle James is describing a writer.
4. Theodora seems to be interested in writing novels.

## AFTER YOU READ THE STORY

### A. Understanding the Plot

1. Gladys Glyn is the name that Theodora uses as a writer.
2. Kathleen Kyd is a writer of popular romances. Her real name is Frances G. Wallop.
3. Theodora has written a romance. Its title is *April Showers*. She sends it to a magazine called *Home Circle*.
4. They expect her to cook and to help with the younger children.
5. Her family is proud of her, other girls copy her way of dressing and speaking, her old teachers congratulate her.
6. She discovers that the story *April Showers* in *Home Circle* is not her story. She goes to the office of *Home Circle*.

7. She finds out that Kathleen Kyd had written a story with the same title as her story, and the magazine sent the acceptance letter to Theodora by mistake.
8. Theodora's father meets her at the train station. He wants to show his sympathy for her.

## B. Understanding Words in Context

1. b   2. a   3. c   4. c   5. b   6. a

## C. Close Reading: Irony and Inference

1. Dr. Dace doesn't think Theodora went dancing the night before. We infer that he's angry that she's late to breakfast. He really means that she should be responsible for her family jobs.
2. She "pities" the great novelist for being so old before she became famous. No, the author doesn't want us to infer that Theodora has written a fine book, but only that Theodora believes that she has.
3. Dr. Dace doesn't want her to take down the embroidered words. He wants her to pay more attention to helping at home.
4. Dr. Dace means that now Theodora will need more time to write and have less time to help with the cooking and other jobs at home. We infer that he is really proud of her.

## D. Vocabulary Practice (sample answers)

2. needed support from their families.
3. not very good for young people.
4. write the book down to the average reader's level.
5. do her jobs responsibly.

## E. Word Forms

1. contributor, contribution
2. critical, criticism
3. intentionally, intends
4. congratulatory, congratulations
5. complain, complaint,
6. apologizes, apology

# 4. RIP VAN WINKLE

## BEFORE YOU READ THE STORY

### A. About the Author

Irving was named for General George Washington. He worked for his brother's business and was American ambassador to Spain.

### B. The Pictures

They are wearing old-fashioned clothing and swords. His beard and hair are longer, his clothing looks torn and older, his hat and his dog are gone.

### D. Skimming to Get an Impression

1. a country village
2. a simple, good-natured fellow
3. His marriage was difficult.
4. He walks up to one of the highest parts of the mountains.
5. He meets some odd-looking fellows playing nine-pins.

## AFTER YOU READ THE STORY

### A. Understanding the Plot

1. Rip Van Winkle lived in a country village when America was a colony of Great Britain.
2. He was henpecked by his wife. He went into the mountains to get away from her.
3. Rip helped him because he thought the man might be one of the villagers in need of his help, and we know that Rip was a helpful sort of fellow.
4. They were dressed in old-fashioned clothing, they looked like figures in an old Dutch painting, and their faces were strange, too.
5. Rip falls asleep near where the men were playing nine-pins, after drinking too much of their whiskey.

6. His gun was time-worn, its wood worm-eaten. His dog, Wolf, had disappeared. A mountain stream was now running down the dry stream-bed he had climbed up earlier. The village had grown larger, his own house was in ruins, there was no sign of his family, the small King George Inn had changed into the General Washington Hotel.
7. The American Revolution had taken place while he slept.
8. Vanderdonk said that Hendrick Hudson, the discoverer of the river and country, returned every twenty years with his crew, and they played nine-pins in a valley in the mountains.
9. He lived with his daughter, began his old walks and habits, and liked to sit in his old place outside the hotel and tell his story.

## B. Understanding Words in Context

1. c  2. a  3. b  4. a  5. c

## C. Close Reading:  Henpecked Husband and Shrewish Wife

1. It might have come from being so henpecked in his house.
2. He could sit on a wet rock and fish all day, he would walk and carry a gun for hours, and he helped his neighbors with their work.
3. The outside. It is the only side of a house that belongs to a henpecked husband.
4. As time passed, her bitter heart did not sweeten with age, and her tongue got sharper with frequent use.
5. She believed the club members encouraged her husband's laziness.
6. There was some comfort in the news that his wife had died.
7. They sometimes wished they could have a drink out of Rip's cup.

## E. Word Forms

1. colonists, colony
2. complainer, complained
3. descended, descendants
4. frequent, frequently
5. philosophy, philosophical

# 5. THE WIVES OF THE DEAD

## BEFORE YOU READ THE STORY

### A. About the Author

Hawthorne took jobs in Boston and Salem because his books sold very little. *The Scarlet Letter* made him famous. Hawthorne writes about the past opposed to the present, moral duty opposed to emotions, and reality opposed to imagination.

### B. The Pictures

The two women look sad. They are dressed in long black dresses. They are sitting by the fireplace. The two women are wearing nightgowns.

### D. Scanning for Important Dates

| | | |
|---|---|---|
| 1. | 1804 | Hawthorne was born. |
| 2. | 1825 | He graduated from college. |
| 3. | 1835 | He published *Twice-Told Tales*. |
| 4. | 1850 | He published *The Scarlet Letter*. |
| 5. | 1853–1857 | He was U.S. consul to Liverpool, England. |
| 6. | 1860 | He returned to Concord, Massachusetts. |
| 7. | 1864 | Hawthorne died. |

## AFTER YOU READ THE STORY

### A. Understanding the Plot

1. The story takes place one hundred years before Hawthorne wrote it, in the largest seaport town of Massachusetts.
2. The two women are married to two brothers—one a sailor, the other a soldier.
3. One was killed in the war in Canada, the other in a storm at sea.

4. When Margaret goes to the window, she finds the innkeeper, Goodman Parker. He tells her that her husband has not been killed in the war.
5. When Mary goes to the window, she finds Stephen, a young sailor. He tells her that her husband was rescued from the storm at sea.
6. Each one believes that her own good news will only make the other woman more unhappy.

## B. Understanding Words in Context

1. a   2. b   3. c   4. a   5. b   6. a

## C. Close Reading: Different Characters, Different Emotions

MARY
1. Mary has learned "lessons of resignation and endurance."
2. ". . . since she had heard earliest of her misfortune, she should earliest return to her regular duties."
3. She encourages Margaret to have dinner, saying, "You have eaten nothing today. Come, let us ask a blessing on the food provided for us."
4. Mary "soon sank back into temporary forgetfulness."
5. She was in a dream-like state; "sleep hung round her like a morning mist."
6. She thinks her rejected lover is expressing "renewed interest" in her.

MARGARET
1. Hawthorne says that Margaret is "of a lively and expressive character."
2. She expresses her sorrow "with cries and passionate groans."
3. Her sorrow is so great that she wants to die, too, and wishes that this were "God's will." But then "she trembled at her rebellious words."
4. "Margaret became more disturbed as the night advanced."
5. She says, "I have nothing left to fear, and yet I am more a coward than ever." She means that she is afraid to hear the news a visitor may bring, even though the worst thing has already happened: her husband has died.

## D. Vocabulary Practice

1. a. *Relating* means getting along with.
   b. *Relating* means telling a story.
2. a. *Nursing* means taking care of sick people.
   b. *Nursing* means getting comfort from.
3. a. *Curiosity* means eagerness to learn about.
   b. *Curiosities* means unusual decorative objects.
4. a. *Long* means far.
   b. *Long* means wished deeply.
5. a. *Resignation* means leaving a position.
   b. *Resignation* means acceptance.
6. a. *Retired* means stopped working permanently.
   b. *Retired* means went to bed.

## E. Word Forms

| | | |
|---|---|---|
| 2. a. grieved | b. grief | c. grieving |
| 3. a. inhabited | b. inhabitants | c. inhabited |
| 4. a. endured | b. endurance | c. enduring |
| 5. a. console | b. consolation | c. consoling |
| 6. a. rebellious | b. rebelled | c. rebellion |

# 6. NINE NEEDLES

## BEFORE YOU READ THE STORY

### A. About the Author

His work took the forms of drawings, cartoons, essays, humorous fables, and short stories. *The New Yorker* included all these forms in its publication. Thurber views everyday activities as strange and "crazy."

### B. The Pictures

The man is holding a medicine cabinet over his head. He seems about to throw it.

### D. Scanning Different Sources of Information

1. Washington Irving
2. James Thurber
3. Nathaniel Hawthorne
4. Washington Irving
5. Edith Wharton
6. Washington Irving and Nathaniel Hawthorne

## AFTER YOU READ THE STORY

### A. Understanding the Plot

1. His wife had promised not to use patent medicine. When she broke the promise and bought another bottle of it, he threw the bottle and the medicine cabinet out the window.
2. He thinks that maybe the clutter is caused by the American habit of saving everything and never throwing anything away.
3. He was looking for a styptic pencil, because he had cut himself while shaving.
4. He was afraid of clogging up the plumbing, or causing short circuits somehow.

5. He wanted to tell his friends to be careful, since there were still needles in the bathtub and washbowl.
6. They fell into the sink and onto the floor when he tried to pull a lipstick out from the cluttered medicine cabinet.
7. He took his friends' towel with him, because the dangerous needles were wrapped up in it. He left behind all the debris from the medicine cabinet, in the middle of the bathroom floor.

## B. Understanding Words in Context

1. c.  We read that he has read in a Consumers' Research bulletin that "patent medicine was bad for you." He is "afraid of patent medicines and almost everything else," because of this danger.
2. b.  If you wrench something "off the wall and throw it out the window," you must have to pull it hard to get it off the wall.
3. c.  If a cabinet is filled with "mysterious bottles and unidentifiable objects," these might be a source of confusion and annoyance.
4. c.  If she has something to do that is not necessarily important but makes her put off cleaning the cabinet anyway, it is likely to be something she likes or wants to do, thus something entertaining.
5. a.  We know that paper falls apart in water (it does not sink or fade "rapidly").
6. a.  We know it "did not seem wise" for him to let the needles go down the drain. Therefore he was worried about what might happen. "Starting up" and "freeing up" do not express this worry.
7. b.  We know "there were four needles in all missing." If they are missing, they must be hiding, not "sticking out" or "cutting."
8. b.  We read that he gets "the debris all together in the middle of the floor," and then he "went away." So we know he has "left," and not "cleaned up" or "ruined" the pile of things (or "mess") from the medicine cabinet.

## C. Close Reading: If Only He Hadn't...

2. d  3. g  4. h  5. a  6. e  7. f  8. c

## D. Vocabulary Practice

1. wrenched    4. lurking    7. smashed
2. groped      5. poked      8. wrapped
3. cling       6. clogged    9. spurted

## E. Word Forms

1. consumption, consume
2. diverting, diverted
3. bewildered, bewilderment
4. disintegrating, disintegration
5. exasperated, exasperation

# 7. A MYSTERY OF HEROISM

## BEFORE YOU READ THE STORY

### A. About the Author

His realistic, naturalistic method was new. He tried to present people as they actually were and events as they actually happened. He went to Mexico, Cuba, Greece, and England in his work as a journalist, and finally he went to Germany for medical reasons, and died there.

### B. The Pictures

He probably wants to fill the canteens with water. He looks shocked and afraid.

### D. Skimming to Locate and Scanning to Find Information

1. In the Civil War, artillerymen rode horses.
2. They were used to pull the gun-wagons in and out of battle.
3. They were often wounded or killed.

## AFTER YOU READ THE STORY

### A. Understanding the Plot

1. The armies of the north and south fought against each other in the American Civil War.
2. The farm house had been destroyed, half torn to pieces by shells and by the axes of soldiers getting firewood.
3. Fred Collins wanted a drink of water.
4. The wounded artillery officer was going downhill toward the meadow.
5. They gave Collins permission to get some water.
6. He went to the well near the farm house, and he finally put the water in a bucket.
7. He met the wounded artillery officer.
8. Only the artillery officer drank a little bit of the water. The rest was spilled on the ground.

## B. Understanding Words in Context

1. b  2. c  3. a  4. b  5. b  6. b  7. c  8. c

## C. Close Reading: "Curious Emotions"

1. c  2. a  3. a  4. b  5. c  6. b

## D. Vocabulary Practice (sample answers)

1. it fell off the table and broke.
2. the children ate it all up.
3. I wanted to go out and play baseball.
4. washing it thoroughly with soap.
5. many years of working outside in the sun and wind.
6. it was too heavy to carry.

## E. Word Forms

2. emphatically  4. observant  6. desperately
3. impressive   5. astonished

# 8. A VISIT OF CHARITY

## BEFORE YOU READ THE STORY

### A. About the Author

Eudora Welty lived most of her life in Mississippi. She wrote most of her books about her southern neighbors. She was also a fine photographer.

### B. The Pictures

She is probably asking the woman for information or help. They are probably in some sort of hospital.

### D. Scanning to Find Information

1. Steinbeck: Took courses but received no degree from Stanford University
2. Hemingway: No information given
3. Wharton: Educated at home
4. Irving: Had no formal study after the age of sixteen
5. Hawthorne: Graduated from college
6. Thurber: School and university in Columbus, Ohio
7. Crane: Some schooling at Lafayette College and Syracuse University
8. Welty: Bachelor of Arts at the University of Wisconsin and then studied advertising for a year at Columbia University

## AFTER YOU READ THE STORY

### A. Understanding the Plot

1. As a Campfire Girl, she is expected to do certain charitable activities.
2. She will get three points for her visit. She could increase the points by bringing flowers or a Bible, and reading to the ladies.
3. Marian is completely unprepared for what she finds in the Old Ladies' Home.
4. One of the old women is interested in her visit, and tries to

talk to her. The other woman lies in bed and seems unhappy with the other woman and with Marian's visit.

5. They quarrel about the flowers, the visit of a Campfire Girl last month, and whether one of the women is sick.
6. She picks up her apple from underneath a shrub. She runs to meet the bus and shouts, "Wait for me!"

## B. Understanding Words in Context

1. stammered: repeated or stumbled over words while speaking
2. bleating: making the sound that sheep make
3. pitched: fell down against something
4. whimpers: small, crying sounds
5. whine: high complaining voice

## C. Close Reading: Marian's Experience at the Old Ladies' Home

1. She doesn't sound interested in old people. She has come just to get more Campfire Girl points.
2. She is confused; she doesn't know what to do or say.
3. She feels trapped, and frightened to be alone with the two old women.
4. She almost said that she would get more points if she brought flowers; and then she realized that she would sound selfish instead of kind and charitable.
5. She is frightened and confused, and she wants to escape.
6. She is feeling happy to escape and to forget all about this experience. The word *imperial* suggests that she is in control of life again, and can order the bus to stop.

## D. Vocabulary Practice

2. a  3. d  4. g  5. b  6. h  7. c  8. f

## E. Word Forms

2. consult     5. proceeded   7. residence
3. extended    6. propeller   8. retrieved
4. intimacy

# 9. THE BLACK BALL

## BEFORE YOU READ THE STORY

### A. About the Author

Oklahoma had no strong tradition of slavery, and Ellison's parents hoped for a life of greater equality with whites. Ellison originally planned to study music at Tuskegee Institute. Identity, race, and racism are Ellison's central concerns as a writer.

### B. The Pictures

The black man probably works in the building. The white man with the glasses looks like a businessman. The other white man looks like a working man. Maybe the man took the ball from the boy, and the boy wants it back.

## AFTER YOU READ THE STORY

### A. Understanding the Plot

1. John and his son live in an apartment building. John takes care of the building.
2. John's boss seems to care most about the brass on the building, his money, and the plants in his office.
3. He believes that if he makes mistakes in his work, Mr. Berry will dismiss him and hire a white worker.
4. The man wants to talk with John about a union meeting; John tells him that unions are like everything else in the county—for whites only.
5. Some white men had burned his hands with a gasoline torch. They did this because he had defended a black friend, who had been falsely accused of raping a white woman.
6. A big white boy takes the child's ball and throws it through Mr. Berry's office window. Berry tells John that if he doesn't keep his son out of sight, he will be in trouble.
7. He thinks he might go to the union meeting after all, to see if the union can help him keep his job.

## B. Understanding Words in Context

1. **a.** to go out and get  **b.** polishing  **c.** become angry
   **d.** say  **e.** get me dismissed  **f.** care about
2. **b.** Have you been working
   **c.** It isn't much, but it's very different
   **d.** See those hands?
   **e.** He and I were
   **f.** I have been at this kind of thing
   **g.** start trying to figure

## C. Close Reading: Implied Meaning

1. **a.** He is referring to the red-faced man, who looks as if he might want John's job.
   **b.** He means that this type of white man usually speaks with a tone of voice that shows a lack of respect for black people. That tone is missing from this white man's voice.
   **c.** It means threatening to hang him by a rope until dead (that is, threatening to "lynch" him; see footnote 7). The man is smiling and seems friendly. John smiles back in spite of himself because he knows the man is joking, even though the subject of the joke (lynching) is very serious.
   **d.** By "my kind" he means black people; by "his kind" he means racist white people. The "things" that can't be changed are the bad relations between the races in the past.
2. **a.** He is so angry at Berry that he is almost blind with anger and with his inability to do anything about it.
   **b.** John means that his son had already experienced racism (the black ball). The boy is still too young to understand this.
   **c.** Answers will vary, but some rules might be: Be careful around white people, but always be true to yourself. Don't trust white people too easily, but be willing to meet them half way. Be ready to work with anyone who is trying hard to overcome bad relations between the races.

## D. Vocabulary Practice

2. f  3. e  4. a  5. g  6. d  7. b

## E. Word Forms

1. quitting
   put down their tools and stopped working.
2. dismissal
   they thought he was doing well enough in his courses to
   graduate.
3. inclination
   the fact that he had recently been released from jail.
4. absorbing
   stayed up all night reading.
5. kidding
   everyone hated spinach.
6. stumbled
   speaking in public made him very nervous.
7. temptation
   it's bad for my skin.

# TEXT CREDITS